COUNTRYSIDE COMMISS

914-2511

07. 11. 77

24. MAR 11.

double copy

PEAK DISTRICT
NATIONAL PARK

S. 2½ INCH MAP SHEET NUMBERS

MINISTRATIVE AREAS (as at 14·74)

e Ordnance Survey One Inch Tourist Map

'he Park District' covers all the Park

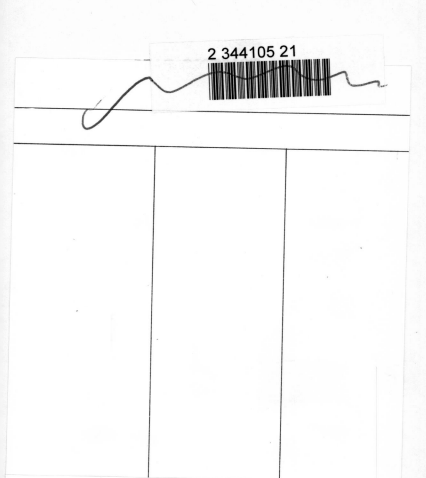

PEAK DISTRICT

NATIONAL PARK GUIDE No. 3

ISSUED FOR THE

NATIONAL PARKS COMMISSION

RE-ISSUED FOR THE

COUNTRYSIDE COMMISSION

LONDON

HER MAJESTY'S STATIONERY OFFICE

1971

*This is a revised version of the guide-book
edited by Patrick Monkhouse*

2 03648800

ISBN 0 11 700497 9

PREFACE

THE Peak District has long been famed for its beauty and during the present century it has increasingly attracted the walker, seeking solitude on the moorlands or scenic pleasure in the dales. Caving, rock climbing and gliding, as well as the mere enjoyment of the pleasant surroundings of countryside and village, result in the area being visited by thousands of people from the nearby towns, and by tourists from further afield. In the meantime, the increase of mineral exploitation and the continued farming of the richer land has sustained the local population, and prevented to some extent that decline in rural population which is evident in many other parts of the country.

Under the provisions of the National Parks and Access to the Countryside Act, 1949, the area was designated a National Park and this brought about the setting up of an authority, the Peak Park Planning Board, having as its duty the protection of the natural scenery and the provision of facilities for the visitor.

This book is a cultural rather than a holiday guide-book, but it is a balanced account of the locality, and includes references which enable the keener student to seek more detailed information; it is the first description of the Peak National Park as an entity.

Since the reader is at least a potential visitor it is not inappropriate to ask for his co-operation in helping to preserve the countryside. Leaving litter, damaging fences and trespassing on private property are common actions for which the visitor is often blamed, and much of it is due to thoughtlessness rather than intent. The Country Code has been published to remind the visitor of his obligations to help rather than hinder the local life of the countryside.

The visitor's responsibilities are reasonable and should in no way prevent him from enjoying the National Park to the full. I hope that all who visit the National Park enjoy their stay and that they will come again.

NORMAN GRATTON,
Chairman, Peak Park Joint Planning Board

CONTENTS

ILLUSTRATIONS

PLATES

MAPS

ACKNOWLEDGMENT

We are indebted to the following for photographs reproduced in this guide:

R. A. Moore (I and III)
K. T. Greaves (II)
Alex Watkinson (IV, XIII and XXI)
T. D. Ford (V)
G. B. Kearey (VI)
Eric Hosking (VII)
John Markham (VIII and IX)
C. D. Pigott (X)
Department of the Environment (Crown Copyright) (XI)
Rev. E. W. Turner (XII)
J. K. St. Joseph (Crown Copyright) (XIV)
H. D. Keilor (XV)
Aero Pictorial Ltd. (XVI)
Peak Park Planning Board (XVII, XVIII, XIX, XX, XXII, XXIII, XXIV and XXV)
R. Gray (XXVI)

The cover illustration is of Mam Tor and is reproduced from a photograph taken by Leonard and Marjorie Gayton.

I

Introduction to the Peak

by THE EDITOR

THE Peak is the last link in the Pennine Chain, the long range of hills and moorlands thrust southwards from the Cheviot and the Scottish Border into the heart of industrial England. That is what gives the district its peculiar character and importance. On three sides it has on its threshold great cities, Manchester, Sheffield, Derby, Stoke-on-Trent, and all their company of mining and manufacturing neighbours. It has in it some of the most beautiful hill country in England, both of the wild and of the elegant kind—and that where natural beauty is most needed and perhaps most appreciated, in abrupt contrast with the harsh, soiled streets of the towns.

But the Peak is more than a landscape, it is a landscape with figures. It is the home of 40,000 people who live and make their living in it or on its borders. It makes its contribution to the national economy; it is a considerable exporter of farm produce, minerals (especially limestone) and—not the least important—water. These activities throw their shadow on the land, like clouds passing. And then, for many decades now, the townsmen have been coming into the Peak to refresh their souls with its beauty. A few make their homes in it. For most their visits are many and brief; living so near at hand they do not need to stay for weeks at a time, as they might in North Wales or the Lake District. They come for the inside of a day, taking nature in sips. But even as they admire, they risk changing what they admire; and another shadow flits over the land.

The task of the Peak Park Planning Board is, as far as is at all possible, to reconcile these human activities with one another and with the beauty of the background in which they are set. Like every planning authority it must serve and seek to satisfy the needs of the figures, permanent or transient, which appear on the landscape. And like all planning boards or committees set up under the National Parks Act, it has a specific and statutory duty to 'preserve and enhance' the natural beauty of the landscape itself. These duties can, if one takes trouble enough, very often be reconciled; sometimes one must compromise or choose between them. Pericles said of ancient Athens: 'We love beauty with usefulness'; and so perforce must we.

The Peak District National Park covers 542 square miles. A little more than half is in Derbyshire; there are substantial slices of Cheshire and Staffordshire, and smaller pieces of West Yorkshire, South Yorkshire, and Greater Manchester, whose county boundaries run right up into the moors. It is, for a National Park, heavily populated, with a comparably large number of developments to command the attention of the Planning Authority. The most populous parts lie in the Derbyshire section. In addition to farming and quarrying, it has itself some scattered manufacturing industry. But a heavily industrialized and quarried segment of Derbyshire to the north-west has been excluded from its area. This enclave includes the town of Buxton, which would otherwise have been the largest settlement. As it is, Bakewell is at once its only town and its administrative centre.

The National Trust now owns a substantial part of this Park, particularly in Dovedale, at Lyme Park, on Derwent Edge, on Marsden Moor, and on the Kinder and Bleaklow plateaux. It shares with the Board the mission of preserving natural beauty; and wherever possible it puts no obstacle in the way of public access. The Nature Conservancy Council owns two small sites here, and has designated a part of the Derbyshire Dales as a National Nature Reserve.

The Park is not all of one character, yet there is harmony between its parts. There are three main strands in it: the high moorlands in the key of millstone grit, which dominate the northern half, and extend more narrowly down either flank; the broad central plateau of mountain limestone; and the complex of softer shale and sandstone which links them together. The moors are sombre in colour, lofty (up to 2,000 feet), barren, often boggy, sometimes heathery, linked by long escarpments or sudden tors of dark gritstone. The limestone plateau, not rising above 1,500 feet and rarely much below 1,000, is a flowing grass-green surface, flecked with white like the sea, and riven by sudden valleys with white or grey cliffs. The shale shows itself in gentler, wider valleys and broad easy slopes. Though so different to look at, the three types of scenery are linked in their nature. They are neighbours in the geological scale.

These contrasts have determined the course of human life as well as of natural history; the kinds of buildings, the kinds of farming and industry, follow very clearly the lines laid down by the contrasting nature of the land. Man has been in the Peak for a long time; we can trace his presence here 4,000 years ago. A large number of settlements existing today are named in Domesday Book—and some of them are not much bigger now than then. When lead mining was in its prime, the district may have been relatively more wealthy than it is today. A surprising number of buildings, especially the manor houses, were built in the days of Elizabeth I and of the Stuarts. Most of the churches here have the imprint of many periods upon them, from Norman times onwards; a number have Saxon crosses, entire or fragmented, in their churchyards.

For all that, the Peak has been niggardly of great men. It has nurtured great families, the Cavendishes at Chatsworth and the Vernons at Haddon, the Leghs of Lyme, the Eyres at and all round

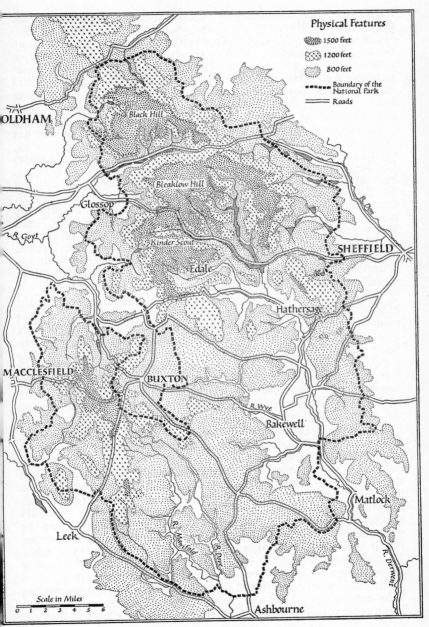

MAP 2. The Physical Background of the Park

Hathersage, the Manners, the Foljambes, the Fitzherberts, the Bradshaws, the Meverills, the Cockaynes. But there is hardly an individual to whose birthplace one would go as on a pilgrimage. There is no Gladstone or Churchill, no Nelson or Marlborough, no Dalton or Faraday, no Wordsworth or Hardy. The best we can do for a home-grown man of letters is Murray Gilchrist, a much underrated writer of short stories and novels, to whom Crichton Porteous pays a fine tribute in his 'Peakland'. But Gilchrist was a Sheffield man by birth, and lived most of his life at Holmesfield, after a short spell near Eyam. Edward Carpenter, the Socialist pioneer, lived at Millthorpe, which is really out of the district, too. Writers like Anna Seward and William Newton, sometimes cited as local celebrities, were very small beer. Charles Cotton (who wrote the second part of the 'Compleat Angler') is better, but not in the first rank. More eminent writers have impinged on the Peak—George Eliot, Charlotte Brontë, Samuel Johnson, D. H. Lawrence, Tom Moore: but never became part of it. Perhaps the nearest thing to a genius who ever sprang from the Peak was James Brindley, the canal builder, who was almost illiterate, but revolutionized the civil engineering of his day. He was born at Wormhill, near Buxton, in 1716. But you cannot make a pilgrimage to his birthplace. It has disappeared. (So incidentally has Cotton's home, Beresford Hall.) Even 'Brindley's tree', which sprang up from its ruins, has been felled.

The Peak lends itself naturally to many recreations proper to the hills. Walking of every grade of difficulty is enjoyed—from a modest stroll by the Wye or the Derwent to the ardours of Bleaklow or Kinder Scout, with which the Pennine Way comes to its spectacular terminus. Rock climbing on the gritstone edges and on the limestone cliffs is a highly specialized form of the art, but has engaged the attention of many first-class climbers. The potholing centre is Castleton; ski-ing practice can be got in Edale. Grouse shooting is still followed by the few; there is plenty of fishing mainly in the hands of local clubs. Details of all these are given in Chapter II.

Of Derbyshire customs, that of well dressing best deserves mention. It has been aptly described by Crichton Porteous, who wrote a book on it: 'Shallow trays about the size of a normal house door are filled with soft clay, which is smoothed so that a picture can be traced on it. Then the picture is filled in with flower petals, grasses, bits of bark, fircones, anything natural, pressed into the clay. Much care and patience are essential, but the effects achieved are quaint and very often extremely beautiful.' Then at a religious service the picture is exhibited, and the well blessed. The custom certainly was first observed at Tissington, but at what date is uncertain. One tradition says it was 1350, when Tissington was thought to have escaped the Black Death because of the exceptional purity of its water: another that it was 1615, when Tissington's wells never failed in a year of drought. Youlgreave has been dressing its wells for a long time, though not so long as Tissington. Many other places have since followed suit, and it is good that they do.

It is more than a pretty ceremony. We have Harvest Thanksgiving for the bounty of earth, and decorate our churches with fruit and vegetables; why should we not also thank God for the gift of water, and decorate our wells with flowers?

This guide is not written, like the conventional guide-book, to help a visitor find his way about the Park, or tell him where to stay. There are other books for the first purpose, and the Accommodation and Catering Guide published by the Peak Board meets the second. It is meant rather for the visitor (or resident for that matter) who finds the country attractive or interesting enough to want to know more of it than meets the eye; to learn something of its structure and its plants and animals, of man's history in it, and of his impact on his surroundings. It may serve in particular the school journey parties which are now familiar and welcome visitors; but it is not intended only for them. Its bibliography points the way to further studies.

2

Geological Structure and Scenery

by J. WILFRID JACKSON

THE rocks of the Peak District National Park consist largely of limestones, gritstones, sandstones, shales and some coals, but the main coalfields lie outside the Park. All these rocks belong to the Coal Age Series or Carboniferous System. In some parts of the Park there are deposits of much later date such as glacial drift, river gravels, peat, and silica sand overlying the solid rocks.

Nearly half of the northern part of the Park consists of rocks of the middle Carboniferous, known as the Millstone Grit Series. With small patches of the overlying Coal Measures, these also border the Park on the east and west, making an incomplete frame to the central dome of limestones.

The limestones are the oldest rocks exposed in the district, and were formed some 280 million years ago at the bottom of a wide sea. Some were formed under shallow water conditions, show the action of currents and often contain much dark earthy material. Others are very pure and were deposited in clearer waters. They are exposed in an irregularly shaped dome about 20 miles in length from north to south and 12 miles from east to west. Together with the flanking gritstones, sandstones and shales they form the southern termination of the Pennines.

The thickness of the limestones is about 1,700 feet, but a further 890 feet has been proved by a boring near Topley Pike, where the beds were found to rest upon a vastly older series of varied rocks. The limestones vary in texture and colour and occur in thick and thin beds, sometimes with a siliceous deposit known as chert.

The succession of the limestone varies from place to place. In the typical section across the dome between Buxton and Monsal Dale the lowest exposed limestones are known as the Topley Pike or *Daviesiella* Beds (from the locality and a fossil of that name). They consist of some 300 feet of dark dolomitic beds with bands of white-weathering limestones known as calcite-mudstones. These are succeeded by 300 feet of very pure grey limestones called the Chee Tor Beds, which are much quarried. Above these are further grey limestones 80 to 100 feet thick, seen in Miller's Dale. The upper part of the succession is somewhat variable. It consists in the main of some 500 feet of grey cherty limestones with massive grey beds at the base in places. They are well exposed in Miller's Dale and especially in Monsal Dale. These upper cherty beds

6

PLATE I. River Dove below Wolfscote Dale

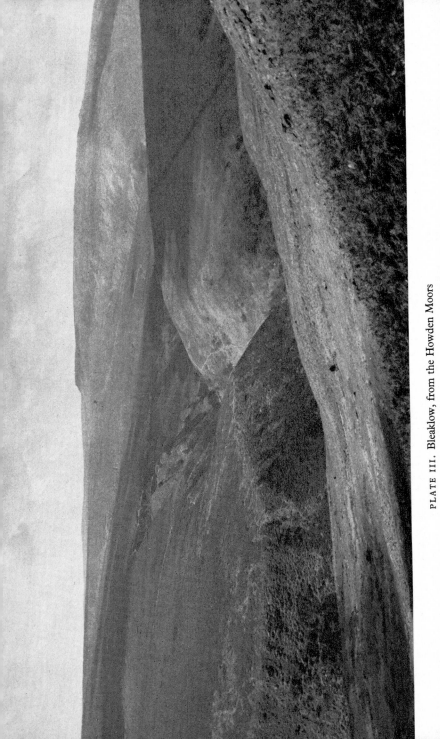

PLATE III. Bleaklow, from the Howden Moors

PLATES IV AND V. Cavities in the limestone: (above) man-made and above-ground—a quarry near Buxton; and water-made and underground—a chamber in a cavern near Castleton

are largely replaced on the northern and western sides of the dome by masses of unbedded grey rock known as Reef Limestone. In the valleys of the Manifold and the Dove, different conditions of deposition have left a contrasting series of limestones.

That the limestones were formed in sea-water is proved by the fossil remains of corals, crinoids, shell-fish and many other forms. These are abundant in some beds, especially around Castleton, Bradwell, Eyam, Earl Sterndale and Dovedale. They vary in size; some very large, some microscopic. These fossils have attracted the attention of observers for over a century and have been much used for the purpose of correlating strata in widely separated places.

The building up of the limestone was interrupted at times by volcanic outbursts on the sea floor. The material poured out is now found as thick beds of dark-coloured rock known variously as basalt, lava, channel and toadstone. Two beds of this material can be studied in Miller's Dale. Other igneous rocks called dolerite were intruded into the limestone in a molten state at a much later date and can be seen at Waterswallows (outside the Park), Calton Hill, and in Tideswell Dale, where the adjacent limestone has been recrystallized and a bed of clay rendered columnar by the heat of the molten rock. Old volcanic vents filled with lava and other materials are present at Castleton, Grange Mill, and other places.

Economic use is made of many of the rocks. The quarrying and processing of limestone is one of the most important industries within and outside the Park boundary and there are large quarries in Great Rocks Dale, Peak Forest, along the Buxton-Ashbourne road and in Stoney Middleton Dale. Dolerite is quarried for road-metal at several places, and chert is obtained at Bakewell for use in the Potteries.

In many places the limestones are rich in mineral products, which fill fissures formed during the fracturing of the beds when the rocks were raised in the form of a dome in post-Carboniferous times. The chief minerals are the carbonates and sulphides of lead (cerussite and galena) and of zinc (calamine and blende), together with the various associated spars, calcite, barytes (heavy spar), and fluor (which includes Blue John). These minerals occur in veins crossing the area from east to west and were originally worked at the surface. Their courses can be traced by the large heaps of debris lying on the surface in long lines. These are known as rakes. Lead at one time was worked on a large scale and is the oldest industry in the area (see page 38). Fluorspar (or fluxing spar), formerly thrown away as useless by the old miners, is extracted in the eastern part of the Park, especially at Youlgreave, Nether Haddon, Eyam and on Longstone Edge. It is used as a flux in the steel industry at Sheffield, and for other purposes. The beautiful variety known as Blue John, found at Treak Cliff, is made into ornaments and trinkets at Castleton. Barytes, locally known as 'cauk', is largely used in white paint and for dressing calico and coating papers employed for process-block printing.

The fine scenery of the Peak Park is clearly due to the character of the rocks and their geological history and structure. Under the action of weathering agents, especially acidulated water and frost, the limestone has been carved into many beautiful forms. The slow solution of the limestone has led to the widening of joints and fissures and to the formation of the remarkable dales or miniature canyons which are a special feature of the area. Dovedale, with its magnificent buttresses, spires and pinnacles, is undoubtedly the finest example of this type of scenery. The river Dove, after traversing the millstone grit shales in the upper part of its course, trenches the limestone wall at Beresford Dale, flows through the limestone country of Wolfscote Dale and Mill Dale, and then enters Dovedale proper, a narrow ravine eaten out by river action and bounded on either side by striking cliffs. The massive wall-like sides are fissured and weathered into many fantastic shapes. Spires, pinnacles and massive towers abound, and it would be difficult to find an area in which so many varied examples of nature's handiwork are to be seen to such advantage. They are the unrivalled examples of denudation by the chemical action of rainwater containing dissolved carbon dioxide. The gigantic monolith, Ilam Rock, Pickering Tor, Tissington Spires, and many others, are especially fine examples of this type of denudation, being pillars of limestone detached from the main mass. Other remarkable features are the Lion Rock, the Dove Holes, and the natural arched doorway of limestone, 40 feet high and 18 feet wide, at the front of Reynard's Cave.

There are some remarkable examples of frost weathering to be seen in the great fans or screes of limestone fragments, locally known as 'slitherbanks', near Iron Tors, in Wolfscote Dale, and other places.

The valley of the Manifold provides supplementary geological features. The river trenches the limestone near Hulme End and near here, at Apes Tor, is to be seen contorted and tilted limestone—a great contrast to the massive strata lower down the valley. At Ecton Hill are the old copper mines, and near Wetton Mill are two famous caves piercing the hillside and known as Nan Tor and Old Hannah's Cave. The remarkable phenomenon of river disappearance can be seen here. In dry weather the water disappears down several swallets, takes a subterranean course for several miles and then emerges at the 'Boil-holes' in the grounds of Ilam Hall. Other caves in the valley are Thor's Cave, Beeston Tor Cave, and Elder Bush Cave. All these have provided evidence of occupation by man and animals in early times. Thor's Cave, some 200 feet above the river, with its imposing tor, forms an interesting study in erosion. Beeston Tor Cave, near the foot of an almost perpendicular cliff of limestone, has yielded important Saxon relics and earlier material; Elder Bush Cave much earlier remains in the form of bones and teeth of the cave lion and cave hyena, together with those of their prey, bison, rhinoceros, reindeer, and others.

Extraordinary examples of limestone scenery can be seen in the upper Dove Valley near Earl Sterndale. Two of the hills flanking the

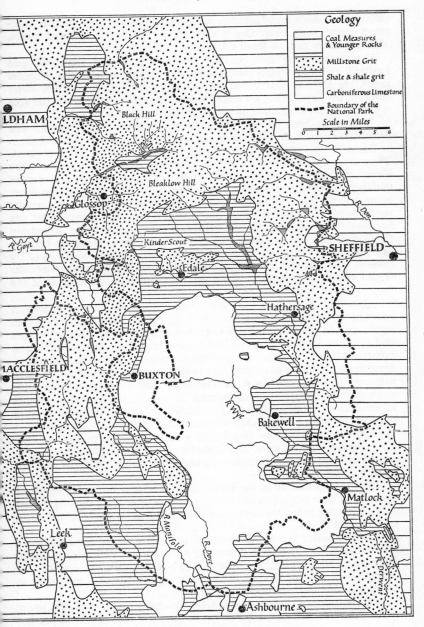

MAP 3. The Geology of the Park

valley, Parkhouse and Chrome, are remarkable for their narrow elongated shape with steep slopes meeting at the top in serrated edges. This region is rich in fossil remains.

Apart from the disappearing rivers such as the Manifold and Lathkill, there are many interesting dry valleys such as the Winnats and Cave Dale at Castleton, and Great Rocks Dale and other dales entering the Wye Valley on its left bank. Examples in the Dovedale area are Nabs Dale, Hall Dale, Hope Dale and Biggin Dale.

The basal beds of the Millstone Grit Series which border the limestone uplands on three sides consist largely of black shales (known as Edale Shales) and form low ground often very wet and rush-covered. They are well developed in the valley below Rushup Edge, the Edale Valley, and the Hope Valley; in the last, they are worked for cement making. These shales contain fossils differing from those of the limestone group. The shales are ancient mud-banks formed by currents which spread sediment over the region formerly occupied by the limestone builders. There is evidence that before their formation the bed of the limestone sea was elevated and the limey mud became dry and hard and much of it appears to have been washed away by rain-water. Later the area was again submerged and the muddy deposits were laid down, sometimes filling up holes and erosion-channels in the underlying limestones.

Above the Edale Shales is a succession of thick sandstones, gritstones and shales, containing fragmentary land plants, occasional thin coal seams, and in places a few fossil remains of marine shells. The gritstones and other rocks were accumulated under deltaic conditions. The hard gritstones form imposing escarpments or 'edges' overlooking the lower, smooth and rounded limestone hills in the northern, eastern and western portions of the Peak Park. These escarpments and the moorlands behind them present a great contrast in scenery to the softer outlines of the limestone uplands, and in addition support a different type of vegetation owing to the rocks being siliceous instead of calcareous.

Examples of Millstone Grit country in the northern part of the Peak Park are the Saddleworth and Langsett Moors, the Derwent Moors, overlooking the great reservoirs (Ladybower, etc.), Bleaklow and the Kinder Scout region.

On the eastern side of the Derbyshire limestone dome the gritstone series is well displayed in the escarpments of Stanage Edge, Millstone Edge, Froggatt Edge, and Curbar and Baslow Edges; also at Chatsworth and Stanton Moor.

Corresponding features occur on the western side of the Park. Here the Millstone Grit Series is present along the Goyt Valley (or Trough) from Taxal southwards, at Combs Moss and the valley to the west, in Macclesfield Forest, at Axe Edge down to the Roaches and west to beyond Wildboarclough, etc.

Of the upper division of the Carboniferous rocks, only the lower part of the Coal Measures is present in the Peak Park. Isolated patches of these beds occur in the Lyme Park area and in the Goyt Trough at Goyt Moss and at Goldsitch Moss. They do not form scenic features, but fossils are to be found in several places. On the eastern side of the Park the Lower Coal Measures are present within the Park boundary at Totley Moor, Big Moor, Ramsley Moor, and a little to the south.

The gritstones and sandstones are worked for building, paving, roofing, and for making millstones, in quarries near Grindleford and on Stanton Moor, as well as in other areas. Some blocks are used for engine beds and for other purposes where weight and strength are needed. The shales are also exploited for cement making at Hope.

Belonging to very much later times than the Carboniferous Period are some deposits of silica sand, water-worn quartzite pebbles of several colours (some indented and bruised like the Bunter pebbles of Cannock Chase, etc.), also white and coloured clays (like Keuper marl). These deposits occupy large solution cavities in the limestone along a line from Parsley Hay to Wirksworth. Near the first-named locality and at Friden, near Newhaven, they are exploited for refractories. The precise age of the deposits is uncertain. The infilling is regarded by some workers as of Triassic age, but others think the deposits are of Tertiary date. Professor Shotton found pollen of Plio-Pleistocene age in the highest sub-drift clay in one pit. The pits are overlain in places by glacial debris containing boulders of Lake District rocks, relics of the Older Drift of the Great Ice Age.

Scattered patches of glacial drift occur on the limestone and elsewhere. They are the remnants of much more extensive deposits left by the melting ice-sheet, which, during the Great Ice Age, spread over the region. Some of the debris is in the form of moraines, as in the Goyt Valley at Taxal, and in the Todd Valley near Whaley Bridge and elsewhere. Glacial overflow channels are present near Lyme Hall and Disley. These drained the glacial lake which at one time extended over the sites of Chapel-en-le-Frith, Chinley, New Mills, etc. Solifluxion deposits and river terraces are to be seen in the Edale and Hope Valleys, denoting extensive wearing away of the rocks and the cutting down by river action.

Classical instances of high-level glacial drift deposits containing marine shells ploughed up from the Irish Sea basin have been recorded from locations at or near the western edge of the National Park. One such site is Walker Barn on the Buxton-Macclesfield road. This was discovered by Professor Prestwich in 1862 and became known as Prestwich's Patch. It yielded some 13 species of marine shells which were identified by R. D. Darbishire, of Manchester, a leading conchologist at that time. With the shells were erratic boulders from the Lake District and Galloway, Western Scotland. A similar deposit of glacial marine shells was found at Cleulow Cross, some five miles south of Walker Burn.

A remarkable glacial erratic was found in 1895 at the head of the Goyt Valley near the old Macclesfield Road (altitude about 1,360 feet). This was an ice-borne boulder containing a Liassic ammonite, probably from the sole remnant of this geological division at Great Orton near Carlisle, or from exposures in Western Scotland, or from the Irish Sea bed.

The rivers of the Peak Park are of considerable interest. On the eastern side the river Derwent, which rises in the northern moorlands, flows in a long valley below a remarkable wall of gritstone from Derwent tip to Baslow Edge. On the western side of the Park, the river Dove, which rises on the gritstone escarpment of Axe Edge, flows at or very close to the limestone boundary for some ten miles and then trenches the limestone near Hartington to continue its course through the world-famous Dovedale. In contrast to the above, the river Wye, which also rises on Axe Edge, flows right across the limestone dome, cutting across the strike of the rocks and ignoring the hardness of the limestone and the present surface configuration. The great depth of the limestone gorge at the junction of Great Rocks Dale is very impressive.

Waterfalls are infrequent in the Peak Park. The most spectacular is the 100-foot Kinder Downfall on the western gritstone escarpment of Kinder Scout about three miles E.N.E. of Hayfield. It is one of the scenic features on the Pennine Way and forms one of the many outlets for the water from the peat-covered area of the Peak tableland. The flow of water varies according to weather. In dry periods little comes over the fall, but after long-continued rains there is a considerable flow. During strong south-westerly winds the water is blown back in clouds of spray. In winter it is impressive to see the fall frozen.

A less striking fall is in Cressbrook Dale, near Ravensdale Cottages (Ravenstone on Tourist Map III). The water flows over an impervious bed of volcanic material overlying limestone and the base of the fall has been eroded by the swirling water. Depending on the weather the fall may be dry. A little way downstream on the left bank is the outlet of an underground stream charged with calcium carbonate which is deposited on the vegetation as calcareous tufa.

3

Natural History

by PROFESSOR C. D. PIGOTT

THE Peak District National Park is rich in interesting types of vegetation and associated animal life, largely because it includes extensive hilly tracts of both limestone and gritstone country. The limestone scenery is undulating and predominantly green, while the wilder gritstone hills have darker tones made up by the deep grey 'edges' and tors, brown heather and black peat. These contrasting colour schemes arise from the differences in vegetation which result from the underlying distinction between the lime-deficient gritstone soils and the more fertile soils developed on the limestone. Both areas belong to upland Britain; a glance at a physical map shows that the Peak District is not only linked by the Pennines to the uplands of the North, but is also the southernmost block of country in central and eastern England that attains well over 1,000 feet above sea-level.

MILLSTONE GRIT UPLANDS

The Millstone Grit formation consists of an alternation of shales and sandstones and includes the massive grits in the upper part. The gritstone itself contains potash-rich felspars set in an iron-rich matrix, but the porous nature of the rock allows a free passage to water so that soluble material is readily washed out of the soil. The shales and the micaceous flagstones tend to be more retentive, respond well to liming, and may produce quite fertile soils, especially under woodland.

Cultivation and improved grasslands extend up to about 1,000 feet in the High Peak, and a few hundred feet higher on the drier eastern slopes above Sheffield. Above this level heather moor, occasional patches of woodland and bog predominate, in a pattern largely determined by the underlying structure of the Millstone Grit. On the 'edges' and well-drained slopes of transported rock debris heather, bracken and bilberry occur; most of the plateaux above are covered by thick peat.

GRITSTONE WOODLANDS

The patches of woodland, though so small in extent, are of great interest, as they represent all that remains of the oak and birch forest which must formerly have clothed all the slopes of these hills. From these fragments we can reconstruct the broad pattern of woodland distribution, for below 1,300 feet oaks and birches grow mixed with holly and rowan; above, oaks and holly are generally absent. The oak is *Quercus petraea*, most reliably recognized by the sparse hairs beside the veins on the underside of the leaf, for above 800 feet the characteristic stalkless acorns are not produced in many summers.

Several processes have combined to destroy the forest, but undoubtedly sheep grazing is largely responsible or, at least, has prevented regeneration when other forms of destruction have been relaxed. We know from the pollen preserved in the bog-peats that an important phase of woodland clearance occurred in this region during the 13th century, and this is marked by a corresponding spread of heather, grasses and bracken.

Later, the demands of the Derbyshire lead industry were met locally; the ore was brought by packhorse to be smelted with wood in open hearths sited on the west-facing brows of the gritstone hills as well as on the limestone. In the past century, the preservation of game on the moors has necessitated the wholesale destruction of predators; voles and woodmice greatly increased, and these rodents efficiently remove almost every acorn in the years when fruiting of the oaks does occur. Birches, which mature quickly and produce abundant small seeds, suffer less and tend to replace the oaks or successfully recolonize open moorland when burning is relaxed.

The woodland remnants occupy boulder-strewn slopes in cloughs or below 'edges', and owe their survival to the rough rocky ground. Most of the oaks are more than 40 to 50 years old and, though seedlings occur sporadically, saplings are very rare. The trees are seldom tall and are gnarled, with their trunks wedged between the blocks; they are rooted in the accumulation of leaf mould and the pockets of rusty-coloured decaying grit. In the glades, where sheep graze and trample the soil, the leaf litter containing important plant-nutrients blows away and the shallow leaching of the surface is the first stage in the soil's degeneration to that typical of heather moor.

Beneath the trees where the ground is well drained, bracken and a fine-leaved grass, *Deschampsia flexuosa*, are common and there are patches of nibbled bilberry. Where grazing has been prevented the bilberry grows more luxuriantly, suppresses the *Deschampsia* and effectively traps the litter and prevents it blowing into drifts among the rocks. Large heaps of twigs and leaf mid-ribs, which have a pungent smell of formic acid, mark the underground nests of the wood ant. The shelter provided by the trees encourages a dense growth of grey lichens (*Platysma glaucum*, *Parmelia saxatilis* and *P. physodes*), mosses (*Dicranum scoparium*, *D. fuscescens*, *Plagiothecium undulatum* and *Polytrichum formosum*) and liverworts (*Lepidozia reptans* and *Barbilophozia floerkii*) over the rocks. The bracken provides shelter for woodcock; mixed flocks of tits are common in the trees, while the older trunks provide nesting sites for the tree creeper, green and greater spotted woodpeckers, as well as occasional pairs of the much less common summer visitor, the pied flycatcher, a bird which breeds only in the north and west of Britain.

In many of the woods, springs emerge above thin shale beds beneath the gritstone edges, and here, as along the streams, alders are plentiful. Large spongy beds of *Sphagnum palustre* may develop if the water is deficient in nutrients and often the small willow (*Salix aurita*) and bog violet are present. More often the water contains dissolved mineral material washed from the shales and this increases the supply of plant-nutrients in the soil. Such sites are occupied by swards of the soft grey-green grass (*Holcus mollis*), bluebells, dense patches of the great woodrush and clumps of ferns, including male fern (*Dryopteris filix-mas* and *D. borreri*), sweet fern and lady fern. The delicate oak and beech ferns occur more rarely under similar conditions at higher altitudes beneath birch and aspen on ledges inaccessible to sheep.

Late stages in the degeneration of these woods can be seen in many places where scrubby patches of birch, and occasional dead or 'stag-headed' oaks, stand on rocks or on brackeny slopes. In fact, the large patches of bracken on the lower moorland usually mark the deeper soils, while heather occurs on the shallower leached soils, and bilberry, mixed with the evergreen and red-fruited cowberry with which it occasionally hybridizes, covers or fringes the gritstone boulders. On these slopes, the green hairstreak butterfly may be encountered during May in remarkable abundance on birches or on the scattered hawthorns, which usually are associated with improved soils of abandoned pasture. The birds of these lower brackeny hillsides include both moorland and woodland species; the nightjar may be mentioned as one rarer species which may be heard, rather than seen, in this type of habitat in a few sites. In the vicinity of old buildings and walls, the redstart is not only frequent but conspicuous because of its orange-red rump.

GRITSTONE MOORLANDS

Woodland has long since disappeared from most of the gritstone upland and its place has been taken by various types of moorland. The extensive tracts of heather moor generally present a patchwork produced by the widespread practice of moor burning. Within each patch, all the heather plants attain the same phase of vigour in their life simultaneously and many of the plants originally associated with the heather tend to be eliminated. This almost certainly explains the disappearance of the club-mosses (*Lycopodium selago* and *L. alpinum*) from localities where they were recorded during the last century, as well as the rarity of such plants as *Lycopodium clavatum*, small twayblade, chickweed wintergreen and bearberry, which linger only in a few places where uneven-age heather, more luxuriant mosses and lichens and the scarcity of charcoal in the humus indicate a rarity of burning.

The birds of the high moorlands are few in species but extremely characteristic. Grouse are the most familiar and conspicuous but more widespread is the meadow pipit, a small brown bird which is readily recognized by the white side-feathers of the tail as it rises from the ground. Several much rarer birds are also present and are of particular interest because they are northern and upland in distribution and are at their south-eastern limit in England as breeding species. Merlin and ring ouzel survive in the more remote cloughs and the short-eared owl may be encountered on the open moor. Black grouse occur in small numbers and the cocks may be observed at peculiar courtship dances known as 'lecks' in at least one site within the National Park. Northern species of insects are also characteristic and, of those which are more conspicuous, the large black furry caterpillars of the northern eggar moth, which feeds on heather and bilberry, and one of the orange-tailed bumble-bees, *Bombus lapponicus*, which visits the flowers of bilberry, may be mentioned. Heather is also the food of the large green-warted caterpillar of the Emperor moth, and the handsome moths with 'eyes' on their wings are frequent in early summer.

Although Kinder Scout is over 2,000 feet high, no true mountain vegetation is developed and the flat summit plateau, like most gritstone tops, is covered by deep bog and eroding peat. The undissected bog surface consists almost entirely of tussocks of cotton grass. In May and June the thousands of fruiting heads, like so many rabbits' tails, explain such names as Featherbed and White Path Moss. The creeping cotton grass, recognized by its several heads and broad-channelled leaves with a solid tip, is abundant in the soakways. On the highest moors there are patches of the mulberry-like leaves of the cloudberry, which however rarely fruits, but only in very few situations are there patches of true *Sphagnum* bog containing such distinctive plants as sundew, cranberry and the bog rosemary. Beneath the surface mat of cotton grass, however, the peat is in many places largely composed of remains of species of *Sphagnum* now rare or extinct. The history of these bogs can be constructed from the remains they preserve. We know that the deepest peats began to form about 6000 B.C., at a time when men of the Middle Stone Age wandered along the gritstone edges and left their heaps of small flint instruments to be preserved *beneath* the peat. Previously the tops had carried birch wood and more rarely oaks and pines, whose stumps are also preserved in a few places. At these altitudes the prevalent low temperature resulting in low evaporation, the cloudiness and relatively high rainfall favoured water-logging and growth of peat, not only in poorly-drained depressions but even on slopes where the normal processes of moorland soil development were arrested by the formation of a hard 'pan' which sealed over the porous gritstone.

The change to cotton grass seems to have occurred quite recently and is largely a result of sheep grazing and trampling. Regular burning favours heather, and some areas have been converted to grouse moor by this means. With the disappearance of *Sphagnum*, except for patches of *S. recurvum* around springs and in pools, where the bog surface is broken it does not 'heal over' and thus channels begin to develop. Water erodes into the soft peat and the channels coalesce and form deep gullies. The peat begins to drain and cotton grass is replaced by bilberry and crowberry; eventually only great hummocks of brown peat remain as on the moors near Holme Moss. Apart from the sheep, the only large mammal is the blue hare, introduced during the last century and now not uncommon. Meadow pipits abound, and grouse chuckle and cluck among the peat haggs; golden plover breed on a few boggy summits and the forlorn call of this bird is a perfectly appropriate sound to the desolate surroundings.

LIMESTONE WOODLANDS

The Carboniferous Limestone of Derbyshire forms an extensive upland plateau about 1,000 feet above sea-level, which is deeply and abruptly incised by the narrow steep-sided dales. Apart from the 'toadstones' and layers of chert mainly in the upper beds, most of the limestone contains a very high proportion of calcium carbonate, so that the shallow soils developed directly over the rock are often strongly calcareous. On the plateau, however, the limestone is widely covered by a brown loamy material or a deep chert gravel, which is of interest because its mineral content indicates that it is partly a residue from the limestone, and partly dust carried, during glacial times, by the wind from elsewhere.

In view of the soil and the altitude of the limestone plateau it is safe to conclude that formerly there was widespread woodland. We know from the refuse near their settlements in the dales that the Neolithic people hunted such woodland animals as wild boar and red deer, but by the Roman period the rich veins of lead ore were already being exploited and the plateau woods may well have provided fuel for smelting. By the end of the 16th century William Camden mentions 'the grassy hills and vales which feed abundance of cattle and great stocks of sheep very securely'. The woodland removed, the deep plateau soils became subject to leaching; by the early 19th century John Farey writes of the extent of heath on many parts of the limestone, and then instructs the farmers how noxious heather may be destroyed. Even today patches of moorland survive, above Bradwell, on Longstone Edge and near Parwich, but for the most part the plateau is improved pastureland, enclosed by stone walls and treeless except for the shelter-belts of beech, elm and sycamore planted around the farms.

LIMESTONE DALES

The rich and varied vegetation of the dales is a pleasant contrast to the monotony of the plateau. Here there are high cliffs of limestone, steep screes and grassy or wooded slopes, where the shallow soils are full of limestone fragments. The relation between woodland, scrub and pasture is largely determined by grazing which prevents or reduces the chance of establishment of tree seedlings. The trees in some of the ash woods prove to be all about the same age, and dead and dying hawthorns of about the same age, beneath the ashes, indicate that the wood originated on an open slope at a time when grazing was, at least temporarily, relaxed. A similar recent phase of invasion of grassland by trees has followed the elimination of rabbits from the dales by myxomatosis. Such ash woods are dominated by ash and wych elm; sycamore is widely naturalized and the shrub layer includes hazel, hawthorn, dogwood, privet and sloe. Ash woods of much greater antiquity are present in several dales and contain a more varied assemblage of trees, including oak in Dovedale, large and small-leaved lime, yew, and such shrubs as hazel, bird cherry, field maple, spindle and buckthorn.

During the summer, dog's mercury forms an almost continuous carpet in woods on limestone scree and is associated with garlic, male fern, wood forget-me-not, wild arum and several large grasses, including *Brachypodium silvaticum* and *Bromus ramosus*. Lily-of-the-valley is locally plentiful. On heavier soils washed down from the plateau above, tussocks of the coarse grass, *Deschampsia caespitosa*, replace dog's mercury.

The fauna of the ash woods includes most of the common woodland birds and among mammals the badger is especially characteristic. Badger setts are frequent in most of the wooded dales but the most easily recognized evidence of their presence are the narrow trampled pathways through the dog's mercury which directly ascend the steep slope and pass beneath fallen branches. The more open woodland and scrub are particularly favoured by the summer influx of warblers and other migrant birds. Of these the tree pipit seems characteristic and is conspicuous because of its song during a short upward flight from its perch in a tree and abrupt vertical descent.

LIMESTONE GRASSLANDS

The turf, which occupies the slopes where woodland has receded, contains an extremely rich and varied flora. Along the upper slopes of the dales, where the loamy soil of the plateau thins out, the turf is dominated by bent grass (*Agrostis tenuis*) and it is in this situation that the mountain pansy (*Viola lutea*) is commonly so abundant. On the steeper slopes below, where the soil only scantily covers the underlying limestone, the turf is composed largely of fescue (*Festuca ovina* and *F. rubra*), quaking grass, small sedges and, over scree, the coarse oat grass (*Arrhenatherum elatius*). In the late spring these pastures are occupied by the flowers of cowslips, early purple orchids and hairy violets. By midsummer these are replaced by rockrose, limestone, bedstraw (*Galium sterneri*), purging flax, bird's foot trefoil, hawkbit (*Leontodon hispidus*), salad burnet, lamb's ear plantain, thyme (*Thymus drucei*), harebell, dove's scabious and Lady's mantle (usually *Alchemilla vestita*). These lime-loving plants give to the turf much of the aspect of the chalk downs of southern England; but several southern species are absent and others, such as horse-shoe vetch, clustered bellflower and stemless thistle, are rare and confined to slopes of southerly aspect.

The animal life though less conspicuous is even richer in species. On sunny days the southerly slopes are alive with short-horned grasshoppers, bees and hoverflies. Among butterflies the common blue and small heath are most frequent and the brown argus occurs in several dales. On these same warm slopes numerous hummocks of fine soil are the nests of the yellow ant. The highly calcareous soil is particularly favourable for snails and several small species are abundant in the turf and in the soil itself.

Ledges on the cliffs and screes offer a habitat for more specialized plants and animals and many of the species present are rare, and remarkable for the disjunct pattern of their distribution in the British Isles. The narrow ledges on south-facing buttresses of limestone provide a habitat for Nottingham catchfly and spring cinque-foil (*Potentilla tabernaemontana*), while red helleborine, meadow rue (*Thalictrum minus*), cranesbill (*Geranium sanguineum*) and limestone polypody (*Thelypteris robertiana*) occur locally on unshaded screes. On the steep northerly cliffs and scree, where the limestone soils remain moist and cool, Dovedale moss (*Saxifraga hypnoides*) and the truly wild Jacob's ladder are locally plentiful and on more loamy soils two other northern species, globe flower and melancholy thistle, are found.

Numerous species of moss and liverwort thrive on these outcrops of limestone and play an important part in the development of the black, sooty-textured soils which accumulate on the ledges and in fissures. Some species, for example *Camptothecium sericeum*, are remarkably resistant to exposure and desiccation while others, such as *Ctenidium molluscum*, tend to be restricted to the moister, shaded situations. Many small animals live among these moss cushions and mention may be made of two which are readily recognized: the large black millepede (*Cylindroiulus londinensis*) and the small snail, *Clausilia bidentata*, with small slender-spired shell commonly found in fissures of the rock. Even the limestone, which at first seems bare, supports many small lichens, including the egg-yolk yellow patches of *Caloplaca aurantea*, *Verrucaria nigrescens*, like spots of tar, and the white patches with minute black pits of *V. sphinctrina*.

LIMESTONE CAVES

Permanent rivers flow through several of the dales and are famous for their trout and grayling, which may be seen in the clear water among the streamers of water buttercup, but many of the smaller dales are dry valleys, or watered by temporary streams which disappear in dry years and find their way underground through fissures in the limestone. In conclusion some brief mention should be made of the natural history of the caves themselves. Plants are restricted to the vicinity of the openings where light penetrates, but a number of specialized small creatures inhabitat the deeper recesses. Caves also afford a resting place for bats and several species, including the lesser horse-shoe and the whiskered

Natural History

bat, occur in Derbyshire. The caves are most remarkable, however, for the large number of animal remains preserved in the layers of clay and rubble which have accumulated in them. Some of these creatures were living in Derbyshire during the long milder phases between the glacial periods of the Great Ice Age, but many of the remains are of animals, such as bison, reindeer, brown bear, wolf, lynx and the giant Irish elk, which more probably date from the last glaciation and the late-glacial period at its close. These are overlain by layers containing animals of the more recent forest period and historical time.

4

Earliest Times to the Norman Conquest

by G. D. LEWIS

THE Peak Park has much to interest the archaeologist even if the vestiges of early human activity are not in the main spectacular. This is not, however, due to any lack of sites, as a close study of the 1-inch Ordnance Survey map will reveal, but rather because the grandeur of the gritstone moorland and its heather cover tend to eclipse many of the earthworks while on the limestone subsequent lead mining has mutilated or obscured them. These sites are in consequence not always easy to find, and to make location easier national grid references have been given in the text and in the list of scheduled sites prepared by the Department of the Environment (Appendix I). In many instances archaeological sites are on private land or in game preserves which carry restrictions during certain months of the year; where this applies permission should always be sought before visiting a site.

The differing geology and relief with its contrasting scenery already referred to earlier in this guide considerably affects the settlement pattern of earlier times. In prehistoric times, however, the gritstone moorlands enclosing the northern end of the Park would have been well wooded and to the south the Carboniferous Limestone would have supported at least open scrubland if not light woodland. It is only since man settled in the area that his agricultural and later industrial activities have denuded much of the area of its native woodland which modern afforestation is now in part replacing.

The earliest known discoveries of man's activity in the area are probably best interpreted as hunting expeditions into the woodlands of the millstone grit and date to Mesolithic times. This evidence comes in the form of scatters of flint and chert implements which are sometimes found where the peat covering has been eroded away. Apart from a few chance finds, including some from caves on the Derbyshire-Staffordshire border, there is little to indicate that Mesolithic man hunted to any extent on the limestone. He may, however, have organized expeditions to the Wye Valley for chert from which he made some of his stone tools. The chance discoveries found when walking in the countryside can often assist the archaeologist in reconstructing the story of the past. He is always glad to hear of such finds which should be reported to the nearest museum.

THE NEW STONE AGE

The first farming communities to reach Britain commence the Neolithic or New Stone Age. The earliest of their sites are found in southern Britain and on each side of the Irish Sea and date to before 3000 B.C. With them they brought the knowledge of domesticated animals such as oxen, sheep, goats and pigs and also seed-corn to plant in small arable plots which were dug in the virgin soil after cutting and burning the native woodland; for this they used stone axes, many of which have been found in the area. The rock from which they were made can be traced to axe factory sites as far away as Cornwall, North Wales and the Lake District.

The limestone plateau which forms the heart of the Peak District would have been suitable to these early farmers with its well-drained light soils, easily managed by the primitive equipment available. In fact we have little evidence of early Neolithic colonization in the area; the reason for this is not hard to find for the Peak would then have been a scrubland island in a sea of forest. When penetration was effected, however, it does not appear to have been along the river valleys as might have been expected but rather over the steep hills to the west. Certainly the Neolithic chambered tombs of the Peak have more affinities with those on the Irish Sea coasts than elsewhere; they are the oldest structures surviving in the Peak and probably date to towards the end of the second millenium B.C. The best-preserved examples are *Minninglow*, Aldwark (SK 209573), *Five Wells* on Taddington Moor (SK 124710) and *Green Low*, Aldwark (SK 232580), the last having been partly excavated and restored recently.

The tombs contain a chamber or chambers constructed out of massive blocks of roughly dressed stone. At Five Wells (Plate XIII) two such chambers can be seen situated back to back across the diameter of a circular mound. The chambers have lost their capstones, and the mound, which has been robbed of most of its stone, would originally have enveloped the chambers, hiding them completely from view. Access to the chambers would have been by passages from the outside and one of these can still be traced on the ground as a double row of upright stones. When intact this tomb can hardly have been less than 20 feet high and must have been an impressive sight crowning its lofty, wind-swept hill. The Minninglow tomb is larger and in some ways better preserved. There are two mounds within the gaunt and dying clump of trees on Minninglow Hill and it is the larger of these that contains the megalithic chambers. The chamber-plans are similar to those at Five Wells and, although there is now little sign of passages leading to these chambers, one at least is known to exist. When excavated, these chamber tombs have commonly been found to contain the mixed-up bones of a dozen or more individuals, men, women and children, together with the remains of offerings to the dead in the shape of meat-bones, leaf-shaped arrowheads of flint and occasionally the fragments of pottery vessels. Green Low had been previously dug well over a century ago by the Derbyshire

PLATES VI AND VII. Creatures of the Peak: mountain hare and ring ouzel

PLATES VIII AND IX. Plants of the Peak: cloudberry (left) and cotton grass

PLATE X. Ash and Yew on the slopes above Dovedale

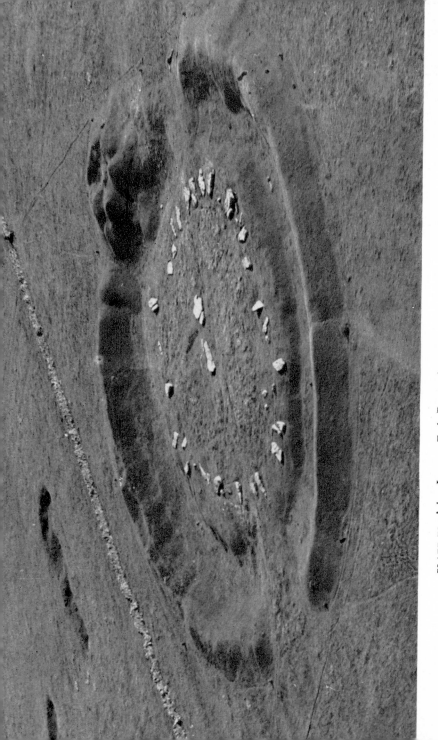

PLATE XI. Arbor Low, an Early Bronze Age sanctuary-site, seen from the air

antiquary, Thomas Bateman, but the recent excavation revealed that there was a dry-stone facade along the southern end of the barrow with a central entrance into a paved passage and chamber. Some sherds of pottery found nearby hint that earlier Neolithic people, probably from Yorkshire or Lincolnshire, had been in the area but there is no structural evidence so far.

Near Wetton in Staffordshire there is an extraordinary monument of this period. Known as *Long Low* (SK 121540), it consists of two mounds, 540 feet apart, linked by a continuous and almost straight bank, 4-6 feet high and 50 feet broad at the base. When the barrow at the northern end was opened in the last century an intact chamber was discovered containing, in addition to human skeletons, the bones of ox, pig, deer and dog. The long bank was also found to be an unusual structure: within it runs a dry-stone wall against which large flat stones have been rested on either side, and this singular means of construction doubtless accounts for its regular, flat-topped appearance.

For a period of perhaps 300 years from about 2000 B.C., small groups of immigrants arrived on Britain's eastern and south-eastern shores. They came mainly from the Low Countries. These newcomers brought with them the single-grave burial site, made distinctive pottery vessels known as Beakers, wore cloth and sometimes used small copper tools. These people seem to have had little impact on the Peak until about 1700 B.C. when, perhaps through a movement northwards from Wessex, their distinctive artefacts appear in the area particularly around the rivers Dove and Manifold and so on to the limestone plateau. Their burials are normally found on the limestone beneath round barrows which are smaller than their chambered predecessors and not easily distinguished from later burial mounds. The burial was normally made in a grave cut into the rock or sometimes in a stone cist and was often accompanied with grave goods. Typical Beaker burials have been found at *Mouse Low*, Grindon (SK 090538), and *Green Low*, Alsop Moor (SK 151554). *Bee Low*, Youlgreave (SK 192647), is more sizeable, being some 40 feet in diameter and 4 feet high, and is at the eastern end of a wood just north of the Long Rake. When excavated last century it was found to contain several separate inhumation burials in rock-cut graves; with two of them beakers were found. A further beaker and other material has been found at this site recently.

One very interesting grave was found in a barrow known as *Liff's Low* near Biggin (SK 153577). A single skeleton was found in a cist formed of upright stone slabs, accompanied by two polished flint axeheads, a pair of boar's tusks, several flint arrowheads and knives, three pieces of red ochre, a macehead made from deer antler, and a small unique pottery vessel. This curious collection of equipment perhaps indicates a mixed tradition connected with the Beaker migration.

By analogy the construction of *Arbor Low* (SK 160635) (Plate XI) is attributed to the later phases of the Beaker infiltrations and probably

dates to about 1700 B.C. It is the best known of the Peak District prehistoric monuments and is in the care of the Department of the Environment. Lying at an altitude of 1,200 feet, it commands an extensive
prospect, especially to the west; from it many barrows, or lows as they
are known in the Peak District, can be seen crowning their respective
hills. It may be doubted, however, whether distant prospects entered
into the minds of the builders of Arbor Low: their intention seems
rather to have been to create a secret place, enclosed by high banks,
where rituals could be performed. This is a sanctuary-site like Avebury
and the earlier phases of Stonehenge, but we can only guess at the nature
of the ceremonies once enacted there. A roughly circular bank, 250 feet
in diameter from crest to crest, and an interior ditch, ten feet deep,
enclose a central area on which are a number of large limestone boulders.
There are two entrances on opposite sides, where the bank is interrupted
and causeways give access across the ditch. The stones lie in a rough
circle close to the inner edge of the ditch, except for four which are in
the centre; all are prone. It is not known whether the stones of the ring
ever stood upright like those of Stonehenge, though since one or two
project from the ground at an angle it is possible that they did so. In
the excavations of 1901-1902 the extended skeleton of a man was found
near the centre unaccompanied by any grave goods. From the earthwork a low bank and ditch ran off in a southerly direction; this may be
much later in date than the monument itself. The barrow which partly
overlies the encircling bank on the south-east side is certainly a
secondary feature.

THE BRONZE AGE

While the Beaker incursions were taking place the Late Neolithic
population no doubt continued absorbing into their culture certain of
the innovations. The pottery of this time reflects some of these changes
and shows broadly a bilateral development. The first of these expresses
itself as the Food Vessel, which may be taken to represent the beginning
of the Bronze Age as its appearance seems to synchronize with the use of
the first true bronze tools in the area. As with the Beakers, the main
distribution of food vessels is on the Carboniferous Limestone. It is
however from the gritstone of Beeley Moor that we have a radio-carbon
date for this type of pottery. During the excavation of one of a number
of cairns on *Beeley Moor* (SK 288688), charcoal found with two food
vessels has given dates varying from 1750 to 1490 B.C., and this may
be taken broadly as the period of the food vessel.

If Arbor Low is visited, then one should see also the fine barrow on
Gib Hill (SK 158633) a few hundred yards to the south-west. This
contained a food vessel with a cremation burial in a stone cist and the
latter has been reconstructed in the hollow at the top of the mound. The
burial itself reflects a fusion of traditions: the Neolithic idea of a stone
chamber being combined with the single grave idea of Beaker times
together with cremation which has Neolithic connexions. Two other

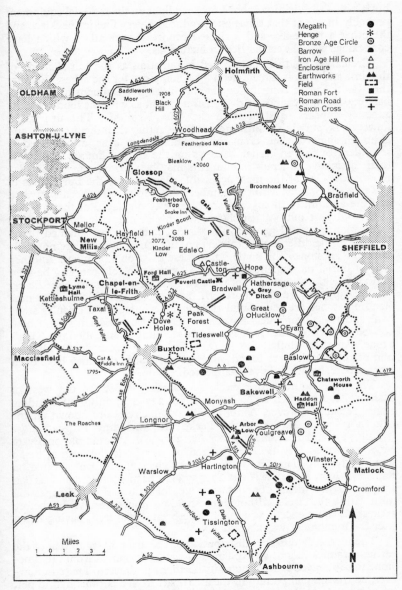

Megalith
Henge
Bronze Age Circle
Barrow
Iron Age Hill Fort
Enclosure
Earthworks
Field
Roman Fort
Roman Road
Saxon Cross

OLDHAM

ASHTON-U-LYNE

Holmfirth

Saddleworth Moor

1908 Black Hill

Woodhead

Longdendale

Featherbed Moss

Bleaklow •2060

Glossop

Doctor's Gate

Featherbed Top

Snake Inn

Kinder Scout

Broomhead Moor

Bradfield

STOCKPORT

Mellor

New Mills

Hayfield

2077 Kinder Low

2088

Edale

H I G H   P E A K

SHEFFIELD

Castleton

Hope

Ford Hall

Peveril Castle

Bradwell

Hathersage

Grey Ditch

Lyme Hall

Chapel-en-le-Frith

Kettleshulme

Taxal

Dove Holes

Peak Forest

Great Hucklow

Tideswell

Eyam

Buxton

Baslow

Macclesfield

Cat & Fiddle Inn

1795•

Axe Edge

Chatsworth House

Bakewell

Haddon Hall

The Roaches

Monyash

Longnor

Arbor Low

Youlgreave

Winster

Warslow

Hartington

Matlock

Cromford

Leek

Manifold Valley

Dove Dale Valley

Tissington

Miles
1 0 1 2 3 4

Ashbourne

N

MAP 4. *Some sites of Historical and Archaeological interest*

burials in of the vicinity Arbor Low shed light on the material equipment probably in use at that time: one produced a very fine jet necklace and the other a battle-axe and a riveted bronze dagger all of which have connexions with the earlier Beaker incursions.

Cremation gradually succeeded inhumation as the burial mode of the time and with it came a need for a container for the ashes. Whether this was the main contributory factor in the development of the over-hanging-rim urn cannot be demonstrated, but as with the food vessel its ancestry appears to stem from the Late Neolithic. The urn users, however, favoured the millstone grit lands rather than the limestone and although some of their cremations, contained in urns, are inserted as secondary burials in earlier barrows on the central limestone plateau, their distinctive funerary monuments may be seen on our present-day moorlands. One of the most accessible places to see the burial sites of this phase is *Stanton Moor*. A number of these sites have been excavated and the antiquities discovered are pleasantly displayed at the museum in the old post office at Birchover which can normally be viewed on application; a useful guide to the district may also be obtained there. Because of the difference of the terrain, the burial mounds are normally cairns of gritstones and some 70 of these exist on this moor. Another type of burial monument constructed by the urn-folk can also be seen here; this is the stone circle of which a good example is the *Nine Ladies* (SK 248636), towards the northern limit of Stanton Moor. The nine standing stones are set around the inner perimeter of a circular stone bank and a small cairn near the centre yielded urn burials in 1789. About 100 feet away from the circle is a single standing stone called the King's Stone. Another similar site is *Doll Tor Circle* (SK 238628) where a number of burials were found; any upright stones that may have been erected here, however, have disappeared.

There is another stone circle on Harthill Moor, to the west of Stanton Moor, known as *Nine Stones* (SK 227625); only four standing stones remain, however. A number of other circles are known on the eastern gritstone moors of the Peak Park, including *Froggatt Edge* (SK 249767) and *Broomhead Moor* (SK 239966). An example on Eyam Moor known as *Wet Withens* (SK 226790) is of one the largest, being some 95 feet in diameter; it has 16 upright stones. One of three on Ramsley Moor, *Barbrook II* (SK 277757), has been excavated and carbon samples suggest a date of about 1500 B.C. for an urned burial beneath a cairn within the circle. Although no standing stones were visible before excavation commenced, a number have been discovered, having fallen after the monument was abandoned.

The markedly different distribution of the urn pottery to that of the earlier ceramics cannot be explained just as a movement from the lime-stone to the rugged lands around its northern perimeter. There is, how-ever, no transitional pottery in the area apart from a curious hybrid pot, known as an enlarged food vessel, which came from a barrow on Gratton

Moor. Early urns are found on Stanton Moor and perhaps there was a subsequent expansion to the north-east of the Peak Park; alternatively there is some evidence to suggest that groups of urn users moved into the area from the north-west. Wherever they came from, and assuming that their burials were made near their habitation sites, the choice of the gritstone on which to live perhaps reflects pastoral rather than arable farming pursuits. Independent evidence, based on pollen analysis in the area, tends to support such a view. Apart from occasional finds in caves the only Bronze Age habitation site at present known is at *Swine Sty*, Baslow (SK 272751).

The middle and late Bronze Age in the area is not well understood. In the neighbourhood of the Wye and the Derwent some bronze implements occur, and there may have been some later Bronze Age activity on Mam Tor and at Ball Cross, both to become fortified sites. However in the absence of more evidence for this phase we must pass to the Iron Age.

THE IRON AGE

How soon iron objects reached the Peak District after their first introduction into Britain in the 7th century B.C. we do not know. Such evidence as we have suggests that there was a gradual transition from the later Bronze Age into the Iron Age. The field monuments of the Iron Age are principally defended settlement sites, known as hill-forts. They are found mainly on the gritstone moors. It may be that the hills of the gritstone moors lent themselves to greater security and adaptability for defence but it is more likely that the people of the Peak continued to live largely as pastoralists, keeping their herds and supplementing this with a little corn growing.

The hill-forts of the Peak vary in size from 16 acres to a little under half an acre. Most of them are contour forts with the defences following the contour of the hill. These include *Mam Tor*, Castleton (SK 128837) (Plate XIV), *Ball Cross*, Bakewell (SK 227691), *Gilbert Hill*, Langsett (SE 206008), and *Castle Ring* on Harthill Moor (SK 221628). Other forts, however, are on promontories where it was necessary to build artificial defences only on one side; examples include *Fin Cop* (SK 175710) and *Combs Moss* (SK 055783). Another defended hilltop is at *Carl Wark* (SK 260815) on Hathersage Moor, near the South Yorkshire-Derbyshire boundary. The defences here consist of a wall of boulders ten feet high, backed by a turfed rampart. This cuts off the approach and the naturally precipitous sides, which have been strengthened in places by walls of stone, complete the defences. The original entrance just within the rampart on the southern side is of the double inturned type, as at Mam Tor. Excavations carried out there some 20 years ago were not productive and it has been suggested that this fort may be of Dark Age rather than Iron Age date.

Few of these hill-forts have yet been excavated but Mam Tor has been investigated recently. Behind what was originally a dry-stone wall retaining the rampart around the hill have been found a number of hut sites which can be seen as shallow scoops in the hillside. One of these produced a socketed axe of late Bronze Age date and it could be that the hut sites relate to a pre-fortification phase. The inturned entrances and pottery finds suggest that Mam Tor was built in the 5th century B.C. Another excavation at the Ball Cross hill-fort, however, has revealed pottery which can be better related to Late Bronze Age analogies. Here the defences comprised a stone rampart and ditch which was originally eight feet deep and on the weakest side there was a counterscarp bank beyond the ditch. It appears from the excavations that the stone rampart had been deliberately tumbled into the ditch.

By the 1st century B.C. two tribes are recorded in this part of Britain: the Brigantes and the Coritani. The boundaries between these two tribes is unknown but it is likely that much of the highland zone was occupied by the Brigantes. This boundary may have passed through the South Yorkshire area as indeed did the later one between Mercia and Northumbria.

ROMAN TIMES

By A.D. 47 the Roman troops had advanced well into Central England. They were diverted from their advance westward some seven years later by fighting amongst the Brigantes; by that time the first Roman troops had entered the Peak District. However, continuing troubles amongst the Brigantes caused the eventual Roman advance and conquest of Northern England between the years 71 and 74. This was followed by the establishment of garrison forts in the Pennines which were linked by a number of roads designed to divide this upland country into manageable areas and facilitate the speedy reinforcement of any threatened points. One such fort can be found in a field near Brough which was once garrisoned by a Gaulish auxiliary unit of the Roman army. This was called *Navio* (SK 181828). The outline of the fort can be traced with its straight sides and rounded corners; but subsequent ploughing of the land has denuded the site and little remains of the fort wall or the interior buildings that once stood there. An inscribed stone found here may be seen in Buxton Museum. Brough was abandoned early in the 2nd century A.D. but rebuilt about 159. It continued in occupation well into the second half of the 3rd and possibly into the 4th century. A number of roads served this fort and these may be traced in different parts of the Peak District. From the south-east entrance of the fort there was a road to Buxton passing by way of Bradwell and along Batham Gate. Another road left the north-west gate of the fort to lead to Melandra, another Roman fort just outside the Peak Park, near Glossop. Its serpentine route which at times is on the line of the present Snake Pass is known as Doctor's Gate. Another Roman road led to the east linking the fort with Lincoln by way of Sheffield. There was also a Roman road between Buxton and Littlechester, a fort close to Derby.

Economically, the Peak District had four known aspects for the Romans: lead, building stone, pottery and corn. Lead was certainly being mined during the reign of Hadrian (A.D. 117-138) somewhere in the Matlock area but so far no mines of proven Roman date have been found. The analysis of building stone used at a Roman villa in Huntingdonshire showed that it was made of limestone obtained from Hopton. At Belper, to the south of the Peak Park, there was a thriving pottery industry from the mid-2nd century until the 4th century. The kilns here produced, amongst other pottery, a distinctive type known as Derbyshire ware. No villas are known in the Peak District but there is some evidence to suggest that farmsteads, particularly later in the Roman period, existed on the limestone, and examples of Celtic field systems probably of Roman date can be seen at *Blackwell*, Taddington (SK 131731).

At Buxton there was a civil settlement, probably a spa, known as *Aquae Arnementiae*, but there is nothing of this to see in the town today except for some remains in the museum. Some of the many caves in the area were inhabited during this period, and vestiges of Romano-British habitation have also been found in rock shelters at *Robin Hood's Stride* (SK 225623). Between Dimins Dale and Shanklow Wood, near Ashford-in-the-Water, there is evidence of another Roman site sometimes called *Horsborough* (SK 168703).

ANGLO-SAXON TIMES

For the period from the Roman withdrawal about A.D. 410 for perhaps 200 years, the evidence is sparse. At Curbar and near Ashover two cremation cemeteries may date to this period, and the place-name *Wensley* (SK 263611) suggests early pagan settlement. On the other hand we may expect a survival of the native population, and the *Grey Ditch* (SK 177815) which defends Bradwell Dale from the north and *Bar Dyke*, Bradfield (SK 247946), which cuts the line of a ridgeway route may be defensive works erected against new settlers at this time.

The majority of the evidence for Anglian penetration into the Peak comes from burials. Two cremations contained in urns, one from *Musden*, Staffordshire (SK 119499), and the other from *Bole Low*, Bamford (SK 220840), could date to the 6th century but the majority are inhumations and relate to the following century. Of these the most important is that from a barrow at *Benty Grange* (SK 146643) which included the iron frame of a unique helmet, now to be seen at the Sheffield City Museum. Sometimes, as in this case, the barrows were specially built to receive the burial but often they were inserted in existing prehistoric mounds as at *Galley Low*, Brassington (SK 218564), where a fine gold and garnet necklace was found. Another barrow known as *White Low* near Winster was destroyed in 1765 and revealed a gold cross and a gilt silver plate, both decorated with garnet and filigree work.

For the 8th century, the field archaeologist will be more than satisfied with the examples of crosses and cross shafts to be seen at *Alstonfield, Bakewell, Bradbourne, Eyam* (Plate XII) and *Hope;* all are splendidly carved in the manner of the period. No monuments of the period from the 9th century to the Norman Conquest are known and indeed the Peak Park has never been densely populated. This short account, however, would not be complete without a brief mention of the fine hoard of 9th-century jewellery and coins found at *Beeston Tor* (SK 107541). The boundary between Mercia and Northumbria was towards the north-eastern end of the Park, passing through the village of *Dore,* in the county of South Yorkshire.

5

History of the Peak

by J. M. BESTALL

THROUGHOUT the Middle Ages and indeed until very recent times the Peak District was a remote and inaccessible part of England; it was therefore not the setting for notable national events. Yet it had during these centuries a place in English life because of two factors which have had a permanent influence on life in the Peak, and which can today conflict to make difficult problems for a National Park. On the one hand, the exploitation of its mineral resources, especially by lead mining, has since the Roman occupation made the Peak one of the oldest industrial areas in the country; on the other, the region has been valued in changing ways as a place for recreation and pleasure. During the Middle Ages the Peak had a special status as a Royal Forest, that is, a royal hunting preserve where the deer and the greenery on which they fed ('vert and venison') were strictly protected for the King's pleasure by a code of Forest Law, enforced by a system of forest courts and a staff of forest officers. Despite the name 'Forest', it was not a wholly wooded area at this time, for there were extensive stretches of open country, especially the 'Campagna' around Tideswell. The Royal Forest covered roughly 130 square miles in the extreme north-west of Derbyshire, its eastern boundary defined by the Upper Derwent north of Mytham Bridge and Bradwell Brook and its southern by the upper reaches of the river Wye to Buxton. Little now remains to distinguish the Peak as a great royal hunting-ground, but two villages derive their names from it; at a central point now called Peak Forest was a building known as the Chamber of the Peak—it is interesting to notice Chamber Farm there today—which was intended to be the Justice Seat of Forest administration, while the Norman name Chapel-en-le-Frith superseded that of Bowden after the foresters had established a chapel there about 1225. A more immediate personal link with these foresters may be found in the parish churches at Hope, Chelmorton and Darley Dale, where their coffins may be identified from the horns, arrows and axes that symbolize their various offices.

The Keeper of the Royal Forest was usually also the Custodian of Peak Castle, established by William the Conqueror and entrusted to his follower William Peveril to control the difficult surrounding country. To some extent its purpose was comparable with that of the neighbouring Iron Age fort on Mam Tor (see page 27) and the Roman fort at Brough (see page 28), from where some of the building materials for the

31

castle were probably brought. The English inhabitants of the Peak are first recorded as 'Pecsaetan' in the 7th century. They were then a tribal group occupying part of the northernmost territory of the great midland kingdom of Mercia, whose frontier with Northumbria seems to have been retained to the present day as the boundary between Derbyshire and Yorkshire and between the ecclesiastical provinces of Canterbury and York. Peak Castle stands in its almost impregnable position a few miles south of this historic border and on the northern edge of the lead-mining area. Its site explains why it was one of the very few Norman strongholds first built in stone rather than in earth and timber in the years immediately following the Conquest. Its most conspicuous feature, the square keep characteristic of the reign of Henry II, remains the outstanding monument in the Peak to a royal visitor in the Middle Ages. From the 14th century less attention was given to the castle by the Crown, and by 1500 it had lost the importance it had as a fortress and a residence.

The decline of the medieval castles was accompanied by the rise of the country houses, and nowhere can this development be better illustrated than at Haddon Hall. Viewed on its hillside from the Wye Valley, Haddon Hall, with its battlements and towers, may at first sight appear as a castle, but its history from the 12th century is increasingly that of a house, the home of the Vernons. Its special interest arises from the way in which it grew stage by stage until the 17th century, so that at Haddon is summarized much of the earlier development of the English house. The old entrance is marked by Peveril's Tower—the Peverils were also the first Norman lords of Haddon—and in the chapel near to the south-west corner is found the earliest 12th-century work. Between these two points the visitor may trace the extension of later building, until the present structure was achieved with its two courtyards divided by the vital nucleus of the medieval house—the hall with its kitchen buildings at one end and the more private rooms at the other—and with the chapel, originally that of the hamlet of Haddon, absorbed into the Hall as a private chapel. It is this process of growth, conveniently illustrated in the angle above the modern entrance where the builders had to manoeuvre to make a junction between the separately constructed north and west ranges, which sharply distinguishes Haddon from the other great medieval manor house of Derbyshire, South Wingfield Manor, a few miles to the south-east, which was built as a whole within about 20 years in the middle of the 15th century.

It is, however, the numerous parish churches which together offer us most visual evidence of these centuries. The early history of the spread of Christianity into the Peak, probably from Repton, is in many ways obscure, but some impressive memorials of this process are provided by the sculptured Anglo-Saxon crosses, notably those of the 8th century in the churchyards at Bakewell and Eyam, which probably mark the earliest Christian meeting places. Such crosses are to be found near the only three Peak churches mentioned in Domesday Book at Bakewell, Hope and Darley Dale. Significantly, the early churches at Bakewell and Hope were the centres of very extensive parishes, in which most of the other medieval churches of the district had their origin as dependent chapels. Except Youlgreave, few Peak churches show much Norman work, but at Bakewell Norman features can be seen in the nave, and outside the visitor can discover how far this church went towards obtaining a west front similar to that of Derbyshire's finest Norman parish church at Melbourne. Why Bakewell came to possess this ambitious church may be partly suggested by its noble group of family monuments. That to Godfrey Foljambe, who died in 1377, is a fine example of work in Derbyshire alabaster from the nationally famous quarry at Chellaston. Upon the patronage of families like the Foljambes and Vernons the elaboration of churches largely depended. At Tideswell, the 'cathedral of the Peak,' architecturally the most splendid of local churches, a visitor asking why so grand a church was built here in little more than 60 years of the 14th century may be referred both to the large monumental brass in the chancel to John Foljambe, who died in 1383, and to the wealth then being derived from lead mining in the surrounding area.

That the church was a focal point in local communications may still be seen from the lines of old roads and sometimes from the convergence of footpaths from outlying hamlets. Royal and noble retinues travelled to the Forest, but more frequent was the traffic between a number of monasteries in neighbouring or other counties and the estates they owned in the Peak. Such estates may be identified by the name 'grange', like Abney Grange belonging to Rufford Abbey, or from boundary crosses, like Whibbersley Cross to the north of the Baslow to Chesterfield road defining a boundary of an estate of Beauchief Abbey, the only abbey of North Derbyshire now absorbed into Sheffield. In the Peak there was a small religious house at Castleton, where the name 'Spital' on the map recalls this medieval 'hospital' or home for a few infirm poor people. Names can also offer clues to the line of medieval trade routes, for instance, a saltway suggested by Saltergate Lane at Bamford and similar names elsewhere, while a medieval bridge like that at Bakewell indicates a road of some importance.

A glance at the Domesday map shows that with few exceptions the villages of the Peak District had been founded at varying dates in Anglo-Saxon times. A study of these gives some glimpse of the English settlers, their reasons for choosing particular sites, or the natural and man-made features of the landscape after which they named villages. The name Tideswell, for instance, which has often been explained by a reference to a well's tidal movements, actually came from the name of a local leader, Tidi, but its ending does show the importance of water-supply, especially on the limestone. Most distinctive of the Peak however are those names ending in '-low', like Hucklow or Baslow, where a person's name is attached to a burial mound. Only one village west of the Derwent, Rowland, has a Scandinavian name, but the Booths in the Edale Valley, which originated as temporary shelters for cattle a short distance from an earlier village, suggest by their names some persisting Scandinavian influence in the district after the Norman Conquest. Again, in the Hope Valley, some places mentioned in Domesday Book, like Hurst, Aston or Offerton, have expanded very little since that date; in Domesday, Offerton was divided between the manors of Hope and Hathersage, and this division between these two ecclesiastical parishes has been continued into modern times. Most places, however, especially those in which chapels and churches were founded, did develop with the slow increase in population in the Middle Ages into recognizable village communities with their extending system of fields. By 1500 the place of Peak Castle, the Royal Forest and the monastic establishments had declined, but the villages, along with manors and parishes, were firmly established to provide the framework within which local life in the Peak District was to go on for at least another 300 years.

The Peak District retained into modern times much of its earlier isolation and wildness. To travellers from the south it seemed strange and forbidding country, made interesting mainly by such natural 'wonders' as Eldon Hole, Poole's Hole and Peak Cavern. Celia Fiennes, for instance, on her northern journey in 1697, observed with some feeling, though little admiration,

> All Derbyshire is full of steep hills, and nothing but the peakes of hills as thick one by another is seen in most of the County which are very steepe which makes travelling tedious, and the miles long, you see neither hedge nor tree but only low drye stone walls round some ground, else its only hills and dales as thick as you can imagine.

It was not until the following century that, as man asserted a more effective control over this region, visitors travelling with greater ease began to enjoy Peak scenery.

At Chatsworth the view today is very different from that of a visitor about 1700. The Elizabethan house, built by Bess of Hardwick to mark the establishment of the Cavendishes there, was then still in course of transformation into a Palladian mansion with extensive landscaped grounds. Over a century later the present entrance and north wing were to be added, but by then the house had been re-orientated to face the river, outbuildings transferred to the higher ground, and the present gardens and parkland created. Whereas under the Tudors a Vernon of Haddon could be called 'King of the Peak', by Georgian times the territorial supremacy implied by this title had passed to the Devonshires at Chatsworth. The wealth and power derived from their extensive estates did in effect make them hereditary rulers of what Georgiana, the fifth Duchess, once called their 'little kingdom'.

In many other places landowners were from the 16th century adding to and rebuilding their homes as their resources permitted, so that today within the bounds of the National Park may be found an interesting variety of these halls or manor houses. They range from great houses like Lyme Hall in the extreme north-west, the much enlarged home for centuries of the Leghs, to those such as the Tudor Hazlebadge Hall, near Bradwell, now farmhouses. A few, such as the hall at Fenny Bentley, still show clearly their medieval origin. Much more frequently they demonstrate the great building activity of the Tudor and Stuart era. Snitterton Hall and Aston Hall are probably Elizabethan houses. Tissington Hall, built early in the 17th century, is of special interest not only as a house but as the home of the Fitzherberts, whose paternal influence, so clearly expressed in the buildings and in the layout of the village, has given Tissington its distinctive character. At Eyam, where the former Bradshaw Hall is now represented only by a barn, the Hall standing on the village street has been the home of the Wrights since its building within a few years of the plague of 1665. Other halls are much less unified in structure as a result of building changes at different periods. Of many examples, Ford Hall, near Chapel-en-le-Frith, may be cited because within the Peak District no house had a longer association with one family, the Bagshawes (now of Snitterton Hall). The homes of such landed families, whose interests were more concentrated in the locality than were those of the Cavendishes, reflect more intimately the history of the Peak District than does the statelier Chatsworth.

There is a particularly interesting group around Hathersage, including Highlow Hall, Offerton Hall and North Lees Hall, closely associated with the widespread family of Eyre. North Lees, standing in isolation below Stanage Edge, is distinguished from neighbouring houses of the 16th and 17th centuries by its strong tower-like appearance, whilst it may be recognized in 'Jane Eyre' as Thornfield Hall. Fortunately it has now been well restored to serve as a guest house. Like Padley Manor, once the home of the Eyres and the Fitzherberts of Norbury, it recalls how this district largely through the influence of such families remained a stronghold of Catholicism long after the Reformation. The same tradition found expression in the early 19th-century Roman Catholic church, unexpectedly classical in style, at Hassop, which was for long another home of the Eyres. No less characteristic of the religious conservatism of the Peak in another direction was the erection at Peak Forest during the Puritan regime of an Anglican church dedicated to 'Charles, King and Martyr'. An extra-parochial foundation, it became famous through its minister's peculiar privileges for the marriages of eloping couples that were celebrated there till 1804. By contrast, there developed in or after the Cromwellian period a movement of Dissent, stimulated originally by preachers such as the Quaker John Gratton, and the 'Apostle of the Peak,' William Bagshawe, and in the following century by John Wesley. Its subsequent progress among the farming, lead-mining and quarrying community is well attested by the number of Nonconformist chapels built not only in the larger villages but also in small and remote hamlets.

Many thousands of acres of common pastures, wastes and moorlands were enclosed especially between 1760 and 1830 under local Enclosure Acts. When this land with a few remnants of the open fields was allotted by commissioners to individual proprietors, they were able to fence their new fields most effectively and economically, as well as to clear the ground, by building the interminable walls that in many places dominate the modern landscape. The shapes of the enclosed fields have their significance. On the limestone uplands around such small villages as Litton, Wardlow and especially Chelmorton the contrast between some of the earliest and latest field-patterns may be seen most clearly: on the one hand, the long narrow fields, whose walls may still by their gradual curves preserve the reversed 'S' shape of strips in the medieval fields; on the other, the rectangular fields, often on the higher ground or further away from the village, characteristic of those enclosed in the late 18th or early 19th centuries.

The straight walls of these more recent fields are often accompanied by straight roads, laid out usually in the period of enclosures and turnpikes rather than during the Roman occupation. Over a wide area roads were then for the first time defined by stone walls and in many places the distance between the walls, including the familiar grass verges, was that laid down in an Enclosure Award. This change made it easier for travellers to find their way, formerly a serious difficulty, which Celia Fiennes, for instance, stressed: 'You are forced,' she said, 'to have Guides as in all parts of Darbyshire, and unless it be a few that use to be guides the common people know not above 2 or 3 mile from their home.' A few years after her visit some of the stone guide-posts with the names of towns cut in each face that may occasionally be found in the quieter lanes, for example near Monyash and on Beeley Moor, were set up to aid travellers.

Later in the 18th century the spread of turnpike roads introduced the modern era of travel and transport into the Peak District and began to break down its isolation. Their making was much influenced by contemporary economic developments and the need for better means of transport, for example of lead, limestone and the products of the early water-powered cotton mills. Although some of these turnpikes, like the very direct road from Curbar to Chesterfield, have declined in importance, the majority are the present-day main roads; thus the traffic problems of Bakewell are related to the convergence of several turnpikes there. The old roads on high ground were finally superseded wherever possible by roads in the river-valleys, but the turnpike era reached its climax in the Peak District with the construction of the Snake Road from Sheffield to Glossop in the 1820s. Many of the toll-houses that distinguished these roads have disappeared, but a number may still be recognized by their projecting windows at strategic positions such as Grindleford Bridge. Elsewhere stone mile-posts survive to record the line of turnpikes such as that from Bakewell to Buxton.

To the inns along these improved roads came an increasing number of travellers, many on their way to the spas of Buxton and Matlock Bath. Buxton had had its important visitors, notably Mary Queen of Scots, in Elizabethan times, but its planned development as a fashionable watering-place dates from about 1780, when the fifth Duke of Devonshire commissioned Carr of York to build the Crescent and its associated houses.

The Industrial Revolution in its early phases made its mark on the landscape. Lead mining and quarrying were intensified. The water-power of the Derwent, the Wye and the Goyt brought some of the first cotton mills into the region. From Richard Arkwright's celebrated mill at Cromford, similar large buildings that by night illuminated their surroundings in a strikingly novel way spread along the valleys to Calver, Bamford, Brough and Edale, and to Bakewell, Cressbrook and Litton. Further to the north-west Samuel Oldknow refashioned the Goyt Valley around his mill at Mellor.

As early as 1848, before the railway had been continued by discreet tunnelling past Haddon Hall and when the station at Rowsley enjoyed the status of a railway terminus, signs of which survive today, 60,000 visitors a year were said by Joseph Paxton to have been carried there on their way to Chatsworth. Railways, as such astonishing figures suggest, opened the Peak District on a new, popular scale.

Their effects on the lives of the local population were no less marked. To appreciate the achievement of the railway builders first, it has to be recalled that although James Brindley, the most famous of canal builders, was a native of Wormhill, near Taddington, no canal ever breached the High Peak to provide the often-discussed waterway from the Peak Forest Canal on the west to the Cromford or Chesterfield Canals on the east. Such through communications were achieved only by railways, the first being the interesting Cromford and High Peak Railway with a line 33 miles in length, mostly at a height of 1,000 feet and reaching a summit of 1,264 feet at Ladmanlow, south-west of Buxton, that was opened to Whaley Bridge in 1831. Built by the engineer Josiah Jessop, this line, which was originally worked on the levels by horses and on the sharp gradients by stationary engines, carried only minerals and goods. Fourteen years later great advances in railway engineering led to the opening of the Woodhead Tunnel and the completion of a line that at considerable human cost overcame the formidable obstacles to communications between Manchester and Sheffield. Some 20 years later the railway from Rowsley was extended to Manchester. Finally, in the 1890s came the line from Chinley through the Hope Valley, largely following to Grindleford the course of one of the canals projected almost a century earlier. Most villages of the Peak District were thus brought within a few miles of the railway.

The map of the Peak District bears many marks of the former importance of lead mining throughout the limestone region. Its extent is well shown by the numerous references to old mines and shafts, their names, such as Venture, Goodluck, Hark Rake and Hazard, often forcibly expressing the risks and uncertainties of lead mining. The veins of lead known as rakes, like Dirtlow Rake or Long Rake, have added another distinctive group of names to the map. A number of old smelting sites, some outside the mining area, are marked as Bole Hills, whilst one puzzling place-name, Calver Sough, is derived from one of the drainage tunnels to which considerable money as well as engineering skill was devoted in the 18th century in an attempt to overcome the serious difficulties caused by water in the deeper mines. Leadmill Bridge at Hathersage, the Miners' Standard at Winster and Leadmines Farm at Elton afford more immediate reminders of the industry.

The lead-mining legacy in the landscape is most evident where shallow or opencast workings have left hollows and banks or mounds. Now they are largely grassed over, but the effect that these scars had on the countryside can be readily imagined, especially since by ancient custom in the King's Field, the Crown land which constituted the greater part of the lead-mining region, the miners were allowed to prospect and work the lead anywhere except in churchyards, gardens and orchards. As lead sterilized the soil and could lead to the poisoning of animals, some conflict of interests between mining and farming was inevitable. In the lives of many lead miners, however, the two activities were complementary, the irregular character of mining meant that wherever possible they combined with it some work on the land; an association which accounts for some of the very small fields to be seen near lead-mining villages such as Bradwell. In some areas, for instance Wardlow and Eyam, the isolated chimneys of lead-mine buildings remain as the most conspicuous monuments of this industry. Such features of the landscape are readily observed, but it is more difficult to appreciate how the Peak District was deprived of innumerable trees in order to meet the enormous demands made over the centuries for wood, partly for use in the mines themselves but much more for the fuel required for lead smelting. The plantations of landowners in the last two centuries have only to a small extent restored this woodland.

The history of the lead miners as a distinct community remains to be written. Here it is only possible to mention briefly that since the 13th century at least their hazardous work was regulated by a special code of laws and customs enforced by Barmote Courts that were translated into statute law in 1852. Although these varied in detail between the High Peak, with its main centre at Monyash, and the Low Peak, where Wirksworth still has a Moot Hall, it may be said in general that these customs and laws defined with some precision how a miner was to stake and establish his claim to a vein of lead, how the ore was to be measured in standard dishes, what payments had to be made to the Crown and other landowners, and in return what privileges the miners could claim in carrying on their work. Barmote Courts, with their

PLATES XII AND XIII. **Two religious monuments**: (left) Saxon—the eighth-century carved stone cross in Eyam churchyard; ... Neolithic—Five Wells tomb, on Taddington Moor

PLATES XIV AND XV.
Fortresses of the Peak: (le[ft])
Iron Age—the hill-fort on
Mam Tor, seen from the
air; and Middle Ages—
Peveril Castle, from Cave
Dale

PLATE XVI. Haddon Hall 'grew slowly over five and a half centuries'

PLATES XVII AND XVIII. Peak styles in building: (above) Jenkin Chapel, Saltersford, erected about 1700 in gritstone rubble; and Lyme Hall, Disley, which contains Tudor work in the hall, although the south front was rebuilt in the Palladian manner about 1720

barmasters, stewards and juries, were for centuries active in dealing with the routine regulation of lead mining and in resolving the peculiarly intricate disputes to which it often gave rise.

Today Barmote Courts still meet twice a year, but in the past century the import of cheaper lead-ore combined with the rising costs of extracting lead in Derbyshire caused such a drastic decline in the scale of lead mining that they now have little business. Population in many Victorian villages fell as the miners were forced to seek other employment. These communities of lead miners, whom Defoe found a 'rude, boorish kind of people' and to whose courage and industry other observers paid tribute, had a language and mode of life which did much to emphasize the historical separateness of the Peak District.

6

Building Traditions in the Park

by GERALD HAYTHORNTHWAITE

STONE is the building material in the Peak District. It was used by British tribes in the defences of Carl Wark, a massive wall of uncut stones, still there and best seen on the descent from Higgar Tor. The Romans used stone in their camp at Brough (Navio) but unlike the British, probably cut the stone into small squared straight-sided wall stones. It may be that the scattered regular shaped stones seen today in the field walls surrounding the camp are Roman. Nobody has thought it necessary to cut stones into such small blocks since the Romans left about 1,500 years ago, and one may wonder if there was not some good reason for the Roman practice. Perhaps a small squared block of standard size might be easier to handle, transport and build with, than the heavy uncut blocks in use today.

All the stones quarried in the Peak belong to the Carboniferous system, but they vary greatly in texture, formation and colour. The most noticeable difference is between the gritstone and the limestone. The former is a rough granular stone varying from faint gold to brown in colour, the latter greyish-white. Limestone is the surface rock of the central and southern parts of the National Park, and around the limestone dome, for that is its shape, the gritstone country lies in the form of a thick horseshoe. There are marked differences within the broad categories of limestone and gritstone. For example, in the north of the district, the gritstone is found in laminated beds which provide thin flat walling stones as well as the well-known Yorkshire flag stones, which are all light gold in colour, whereas at the southern edges of the gritstone country the stone is amorphous, darker in colour and is quarried and used in thick random shapes. There is a similar variety of formation in the limestone. It is this variety in formation and colour of stone which gives rise to marked local characteristics in Peak District building. Around the northern edges of the Peak District, at Saddleworth, Marsden and Meltham the long, narrow, bedded stones give a characteristic fine edge to buildings and made it easy to build the long ranges of weavers' windows. These windows gave a pattern for the treatment of the Holme Moss Television Station which the B.B.C. built so carefully in 1950 (albeit on too wild a site, an incongruous building in a National Park). The greater part of Peak building, and that which is most characteristic of the northern parts of the Park, is in the large shapeless blocks of amorphous gritstone which is built thick and random into walls. Along the great sweep of the Derwent Valley and its tributaries the Ashop and the Noe, the gritstone random rubble clothes the countryside in farms, villages, manor halls and in bridges, and also in the walls which divide the fields and border the roads and which seem to lace together the isolated buildings of the countryside.

Gritstone is squared and cut to make window sills, heads and jambs and other dressings as they are called; and, with difficulty, it is even moulded. The success of the masons' perseverance in dealing with this hard unresponsive stone can be seen in the door and window surrounds in the manor halls which abound in the Derwent Valley.

Along the edge of the limestone country where the limestone turns to shale and then disappears under the gritstone cap, there are a number of towns and villages where both kinds of surface rock have been available for building, the more important ones being Hulme End, Hartington, Longnor, Buxton, Sparrowpit, Chapel-en-le-Frith, Castleton, Hucklow, Eyam, and Bakewell. The difference in appearance is marked where both kinds of stone are used in buildings next to each other, or, as sometimes happens, where both are used in the same building. The grey-white limestone is a very different substance from the gritstone. For the most part it is quarried in shapeless blocks, smaller blocks than the gritstone, but, like it, built thick and random into walls. The most characteristic feature of the limestone country is the dry-stone walls, which are very thick, about 3 feet 6 inches or more at the base, and built in small stones taken from the fields. There are a few isolated quarries where stone is quarried in laminated beds after the fashion of the Yorkshire gritstone flags, but the stone is now seldom used. Limestone rubble is a very difficult stone to build into either dry or mortared walls. After the last war it began to look as if no more limestone buildings would be erected, which would have been an architectural tragedy, for nothing else would suit the limestone country landscape. Fortunately a method of making blocks with pieces of limestone in the face has been devised. These blocks are now being used extensively.

Gritstone is used for roof-covering as well as for walls. Certain beds of these stones near the surface have been split into thin plates which make ideal if heavy slates. Ideal because they perfectly satisfy the eye and once in position keep out the weather as long as the roof timber lasts. They are called locally 'grey slate' and they are used in both the gritstone and limestone country. These slates are very large and thick, often as much as 3 feet wide by 3 feet 6 inches long and $1\frac{1}{2}$ inches thick and are held in position by oak pegs, or in the older buildings by sheep's bones. The size and weight of the slates account for the low pitch of the roofs. If the pitch were more than 35° the heavy slates might break away from their moorings.

In the Staffordshire part of the limestone country, a dark blue tile is used instead of gritstone slates. These are called generally 'Staffordshire blues' and they make a good roof of a colour and texture which fits the limestone landscape very well.

The Peak is a mountainous country and enjoys rough weather. This has a marked effect on its traditional buildings, which as far as possible were designed to keep the weather out, and to prevent the wind getting hold of the structure. Eaves were made with little projection and it was unusual to build gutters. Sometimes these have been added and supported on wrought iron brackets driven into the wall. Entrances were guarded by solid and comfortable porches. Roofs were pitched to shed rain and snow. Gable ends were protected by continuing the wall up above the level of the slate verges for 12 inches or so and capping it with a weathered and moulded coping stone. These gable parapets might have a finial at the apex and moulded corbel stones at the eaves.

Each succeeding age provided its own architectural variations but did not depart from the basic traditions in Peak District building. Haddon Hall, the most interesting and romantic of all the buildings in the Peak, grew slowly over five and a half centuries, passing from its Norman beginnings through all the native phases of architectural style: early English, Decorated and Perpendicular Gothic, Tudor and early Elizabethan renaissance. It appears to have had chambers added as each succeeding generation of the Vernons prospered, up to the building of the Long Gallery in about 1600 by the then new owner Sir John Manners. For each addition the builders took advantage of the new thoughts in design and the new methods of construction which were current at the time, but so submitted to the natural conditions of the site that each new part was perfectly related to the existing buildings and to the landscape. Perhaps the two most stringent of the natural conditions of any site are the shape of the ground and the nature of the building material closest at hand. If a builder gives full consideration to the shape of the ground and fully adapts his building thereto and uses local materials for his work, it seems reasonable to expect that the natural characteristics of the site will be reflected in the building. This is particularly the case when the local building material is the surface rock of the country. It is so at Haddon Hall where the building seems to enhance the magnificent scenery along the banks of the river Wye.

One and a half miles south of Haddon Hall, the rivers Wye and Derwent flow together at Great Rowsley. Between their separate sources in the north of the National Park and their confluence at Rowsley are the most accessible and the best of Peak District buildings. The buildings along the banks of the Derwent are gritstone and most of those along the Wye are limestone. Three miles up the Derwent from Rowsley is Chatsworth, set in a made-up landscape with the river tamed and made sleepy by Capability Brown. This ducal mansion was built in a bold Italian manner by several architects over a period of 140 years and was started by William Talman in 1690. It is an exercise in self-conscious art and stands aloof from the life of the Peak District; but it does no violence to the countryside for it takes full account of the shape of the site and it is built in local gritstone. The only other important mid- or late-renaissance mansion in the National Park is

Lyme Hall. It lies on the western boundary of the Park in Cheshire, and like Chatsworth is built of local gritstone. The south front of the hall was built in the Palladian manner by Giacomo Leoni in 1720, but on the north front there is an unusually interesting early Elizabethan renaissance gateway built about 1570. It is interesting to compare the different forms of renaissance architecture in the two fronts, in time 150 years apart.

Further northwards along the river Derwent on either bank within $1\frac{1}{2}$ miles of the river there are a succession of fine halls built of gritstone with grey slate roofs: Bubnell Hall (16c), Hassop Hall (16c), Eyam Hall (17c), Hazelford Hall (17c), Highlow Hall (16c), North Lees Hall (16c) and Offerton Hall (16c). The last three lie about $1\frac{1}{2}$ miles from Hathersage and were reputedly founded by Nicholas Eyre of Hope for his sons in the reign of Henry IV. Their architectural styles, however, show them to be Elizabethan and Jacobean manors, although they may be of an earlier foundation.

The Wye Valley manor halls and country houses are not so easily approached as those of the Derwent. The valley is narrow and deepens towards its source into steep-sided and often cliff-lined dales. In the wider parts is the township of Bakewell, on the north-west side of which is Holme Hall (1626), one of the best of the limestone halls.

Beyond the Wye and Derwent country there are buildings to enjoy. Churches, castles, manors, farmsteads and town houses, market halls and village crosses, dovecotes and bridges: all built of the local stone and all combining to proclaim the truth that new thoughts in building give life and beauty to the landscape so long as the natural forms and colours of the site are respected. It is a self-evident truth that unless a building responds to the dominant characteristics of the land—its colour, texture, shape—it will not enhance the beauty of the landscape.

The $2\frac{1}{2}$-inch Ordnance Survey maps show the situation of all the historic buildings of the National Park.

7

Farming in the Park

by I. H. MORTEN

THE farming of the Peak revolves round grass and its use by livestock, but the kind of use varies a great deal.

The more productive parts of the Park—in the south, and in the valley bottoms—where there is a good depth of soil, have always had some arable land, varying in extent over the years according to the economic state of farming. This no doubt determined the siting of the old corn mills, generally water-driven. Many of them have unfortunately disappeared, but a few remain, as at Brough. In these areas farming is more intensive, and is often devoted to milk production and the fattening of sheep and cattle. On higher land we find the farmsteads in the valleys or part way up the hill surrounded by varying amounts of enclosed land or 'intake', which has been 'taken in' from the hill and moorland areas; by controlled grazing, ploughing, fertilizing, and so on, its whole appearance and botanical composition has changed, especially to provide winter feed for cattle and sheep. In the lower-lying areas one may find these fields fenced with hedges, the 'brushing' of which is a precious rural craft. Higher up, limestone and gritstone walls are the rule—literally miles and miles of them, standing as a fine monument to the industry of our forefathers and to their skill in another precious rural craft. The size of fields tends to increase as one goes further from the farm buildings until, in the moorland areas, we may have thousands of acres unfenced.

Most of our farmsteads have been established for two hundred years or more; often one need not look very far for the quarry from which the stone was won to build them. Small farms are common; over 60% of the holdings are of less than 50 acres and very few exceed 250 acres.

In the limestone areas the poor water supply makes intensive stocking difficult; consequently large fields bounded by stone walls are common. Water schemes are gradually being introduced to amend this state of affairs. There is a clear-cut difference between the types of farming on gritstone and limestone soils. The latter are traditionally stock-grazing areas and often difficult or impossible to plough. The true hill and moorland areas are used primarily—some of them only—for sheep grazing; the heather moors are also of importance for grouse. It is, however, vital for cattle also to graze moorland where possible—indeed, by mixed grazing of both cattle and sheep, controlled where possible, upland grassland can be maintained and improved without

44

spending much except for some form of lime to counteract the often sour acid soils, with perhaps small application of phosphates.

During the war, more cattle were set to graze on the hills in order to free lowland areas for cropping. The rehabilitation of upland areas was enormously hastened by the Hill Farming Act of 1945 and later by the Livestock Rearing Act, the Farm Improvement Scheme and the Marginal Production Scheme. We now see green and intensively used grassland as high up as Win Hill, just over 1,500 feet.

The nature of much of the land in the north, north-west and north-east of the Park is such as to make it predominantly sheep grazing. Long ago there would be some cheese making. This is no longer carried out to any significant extent, but the large stone presses are often to be found in farmyards. One factory at Hartington does, however, still continue and there is produced a very fine Stilton, some of which finds its way into the Royal Household.

Of the cattle, the well-known dual-purpose Shorthorn is one of the most important, but Friesians and Ayrshires may predominate in milk-producing areas. The Shorthorn, in its variety of colour, is well suited to our conditions, being capable of useful milk production as well as beef, and is found pure as well as crossed with beef types, such as the Hereford and Aberdeen Angus. Such cross-bred animals are either reared and fattened off on the lower-lying land or, more often, sold as store stock for the grazing lands of the Midlands, or for winter feeding in the eastern counties. Friesian steers and heifers are also now finding favour with beef producers. In many places the predominantly milk-producing farms are becoming reservoirs of beef-type calves for rearing in upland areas.

Certain other breeds have recently appeared in the Peak, in response to the need for more home-produced beef. We now see Galloway and Galloway Cross cattle grazing on such uplands as Win Hill and Crook Hill. The Galloway is a hardy beef-producing type from Scotland and is kept in the Peak on the suckler-herd principle, the calf usually running with its mother on the hill, at least for the summer months. The north country beef-type of Shorthorn is also used in this way; we may well see more of this practice, especially when Aberdeen Angus bulls are crossed with Shorthorns to give the very popular polled grazing type. More recently there has been an introduction of the French Charollais for crossing with existing breeds, for beef production—the young being readily recognizable by their mushroom colour.

Milk is usually sold through the Milk Marketing Board or, near villages and hamlets, retailed by the farmers themselves. Cattle from upland farms are mainly sold as store animals in spring or autumn, some privately, others through the cattle markets, particularly at Bakewell, and also at the traditional fairs. (Fairs established long ago still continue, as at Hope and Newhaven; others may be revived with the probable increase of young cattle for disposal in the Peak.)

Over a vast area of the Peak sheep are of greatest importance. Most important numerically are the hill breeds, among which our Derbyshire Gritstone still predominates, ranging through north-east Staffordshire and Cheshire and north Derbyshire as far as the Yorkshire borders, and extending also northwards into Lancashire. The Gritstone is well known as an active sheep, well able to withstand the rigours of the climate and capable of useful production from the food available. It is a breed of some antiquity, almost certainly descended from the old 'Dale of Goyt' sheep and improved through the ages. The Gritstone can be readily recognized as a fair-sized sheep for a hill breed, with a speckled face and without horns. Next in numbers is the Swaledale—smaller than the Gritstone, with horns and greyish nose on a black face. The ewe is a particularly good mother. One should also mention the Scotch Blackface, of which there are a few flocks—a horned sheep with distinct black face and slightly 'roman nose'—and the Lonk, which resembles the Gritstone in many ways but is slightly larger and has horns. The Whitefaced Woodland, a whitefaced horned sheep of great antiquity, was formerly very common in the High Peak. It is very hardy, but slow to mature. This has probably accounted for its decline, but it is still found, and the rams are used for crossing with smaller breeds. On the lower ground, heavier breeds are kept, such as the Kerry Hill and a few flocks of Cluns and Hampshires. These sheep need better food and kinder weather, and are much more dependent on supplementary feeding than the hill breeds.

We have no commons in the Peak, as have many other upland areas of the British Isles; but we have vast areas of moorland suitable only for sheep, the grazing rights on which are very ancient and often associated with possession of farms in the valleys or reclaimed parts of the moorland. Sheep belonging to many owners graze the same acres and a 'code of honour,' as it were, has been evolved in their management. The marks of the several owners are almost sacred possessions dating back a long way and often attached to the farm rather than the farmer. These take various forms: marks on the fleece, burns on the horn, characteristic holes in the ears, or a combination of these. The marks are all recorded in the 'Sheepherds books' produced by the Sheepherds Societies for the various districts, known as liberties. These societies all have meetings during the year, primarily to sort out straying sheep and discuss other relevant topics. The Strines Meet has been going on for scores of years.

A shepherd's life may be hard and exacting of time, but it is one of the most satisfying. He knows every individual sheep and must try to anticipate their needs. He strives to work with nature, but must always be ready for nature to turn against him, by some affliction or in snowstorms, which may bury scores of sheep. Their rescue is then enormously helped by good dogs able to scent the sheep through the snowdrifts. Indeed, it is impossible to think of the shepherd without his dogs, and what precious dogs they are, carefully bred and well trained; as one watches the dogs working the sheep in day-to-day life, it is easy to see why our Park is the home of many famous sheep-dog trials—like Longshaw, Hope, Bamford, Macclesfield Forest—made famous by such names as Elliot, Eyre, Ollerenshaw and Priestly with their dogs. Many are the stories told of hard winters and other difficulties, and so many of them hinge on the understanding that exists between the shepherd and his dogs—best symbolized in the simple but none the less moving memorial to Joe Tagg in Derwent.

Normally hill sheep are wild and certainly not too well disposed to strangers. Yet at certain places, like the Cat and Fiddle and Monsal Head, they are so tame that they will share a meal with visitors or even jump into a car if given half a chance. This friendliness is entirely due to the sheep's desire for certain minerals, deficient in its grazing, but probably to be found associated with man's food.

Grouse and grouse shooting are part of the scene and part of the economy of the countryside; but in recent times the relative value of sheep grazing as against grouse shooting has materially changed. The old pageantry of the 'glorious Twelfth' is largely gone, but to some extent the sport is carried on by landowners, farmers and shooting syndicates. It has, however, been shown that it is by no means impossible for grouse shooting and sheep grazing to be carried on happily together.

Poultry are often kept, but gone are the days of the barn door fowl, and of the hen and chickens. Many poultry are now maintained either on the battery system or the deep-litter system. A few farms still carry poultry on free range, but there are few areas in the Park where poultry are more than a sideline. Tideswell has long been of importance for its poultry and it is still possible to find them on free range in that area, while Great Longstone has an important poultry-breeding establishment and hatchery.

The horse has, in the Peak as elsewhere, given way to the internal combustion engine for better or worse. Many jobs on farms could still be economically carried out by horses, but horsemen are rare. Once the Peak was the home of some of the finest shire horses, some of the limestone land being particularly suitable for breeding and rearing. Now the sight of a working horse is almost an event, except in parts of Cheshire and in the Hope Valley. There has, however, been a revival of interest in riding ponies, particularly for children. This is a welcome trend and to see our bridlepaths once again in their historic role would enrich our countryside, and indeed pony trekking may well soon be a characteristic and highly desirable feature of our National Park.

Bakewell Show is the great event of the farming year, but the smaller shows at Hope and Hathersage should not be overlooked. Other events of rural origin are the sports at Longnor and Hartington, where some horse racing may still be seen. The horse trials recently started at Chatsworth are a new and promising venture. There are also pony club rallies for young people. But it is perhaps in the Young Farmers' Club movement, very strong in the Peak, that we have the potential of greatest good. Here rural interests are encouraged in friendly association and also competition by young people from villages and towns; there are lectures, courses in rural crafts, proficiency tests, etc., as well as social gatherings. In Derbyshire the Young Farmers' Club movement is now working in active association with the Youth Hostels and Ramblers' Associations to promote better understanding between town and country.

The planning picture in the Peak is fundamental to any conception of our Park and the maintenance and conservation of uplands and lowlands is the concern of those who administer, those who live in and those who visit the hills and dales. It is a matter of concern to many that nationally our land is disappearing all too fast. This is inevitably resulting in greater demands on the remaining acres, and we are likely to see 'multiple' use of land—here in the Peak we have already shown this to be practicable, as with walking, shooting and sheep on the moorland areas. This welding of interests is a realistic development, so long as farming remains fundamental.

A thriving agriculture is an integral factor in maintaining the landscape we love, but its retention calls for a never-ending fight in face of odds, such as over-population and the demands of industry, particularly for mineral extraction, road making and water supply, not to mention housing pressures. All of these change the traditional landscape, rarely if ever for the better. The time is fast approaching when decisions must be taken at the highest level to secure a policy of conservation designed to maintain the character of our national parks.

The pattern of farming is already changing; there is a pronounced trend towards large holdings, encouraged by Government policy but not contributing to the maintenance of our upland landscape. The field pattern is vanishing with neglect or disappearance of walls and hedges, and this leads to diminishing animal and plant habitats. Older farm buildings are abandoned in favour of the large 'umbrella' buildings which have a disastrous effect on the appearance of our countryside. Being therefore neglected, these older buildings with the housesteads become redundant to the needs of the more extensive farming. The old farmsteads are ready prey to the commuter whose means so often exceed those of the rural population. Indeed commuter and other housing pressures on certain areas of the Peak Park are a formidable challenge. There is the added problem of requests to convert the disused buildings into houses; while considering each application on its merits, the National Park Authority has made clear its dislike of this change of use, so often contrary to its development control policy.

The fine scenery of the Park can be maintained only by careful integration of farming, forestry and recreation, so multiple use is likely to increase—carefully managed, this need not be feared. Indeed the Peak has already pioneered this aspect of land use in the access agreements now covering some 76 square miles, where the traditional sheep and cattle grazing and grouse shooting continue, but opportunities for freedom to roam are readily available.

8

Industry in the Park Today

THE Peak has more people living in it than any other National Park (about 13 to every hundred acres). Distribution of population is very uneven and some extensive areas of moorland are completely uninhabited. The lower valleys have quite large settlements and many of these support industries as well as farming activities.

The most obvious of these industries to the visitor is mining and quarrying. This is a long-established industry in the Peak District and lead has been mined in the area since at least Roman times. The character of the industry has changed greatly over the past hundred years. At the start of the 19th century lead mining and limestone working were widespread but each operation was small in scale, often being a part-time family occupation. The lead was smelted in the district and transported to the developing industrial areas. The first stages of this journey were often by packhorse. Limestone was burnt in small kilns, often near farmsteads, to produce lime for improving pasture.

The lead industry has now disappeared but the old lead-working areas are now being reworked for fluorspar. That was formerly a waste product from lead production, now lead is a by-product of fluorspar processing! Fluorspar is obtained in three major ways—by underground mining, by opencast excavation and by reworking the old lead waste dumps. It is used for two major purposes: 'Metallurgical' grade material is used as a flux in steel manufacture; 'Chemical' grade material is the major source of industrial fluorine which is a vital part of many industrial processes. Both these grades of material are produced at Cavendish Mill near Stoney Middleton which together with two associated mines employs about 400 people. Material from Cavendish Mill is sent all over the world and, together with other processing plants using material from the Park, accounts for about 75% of the fluorspar produced in this country.

The by-products of fluorspar production are lead, barytes (used mainly as a drilling 'mud' in North Sea oil exploration) and 'tailings'. Tailings are the unusable materials left after the processing operation. Because the ore has to be ground to small sizes to separate off the impurities and leave high-purity fluorspar, the tailings are very small solid particles in suspension in water. To dispose of this material means that large lagoons have to be constructed because the material is too unstable to be disposed of in any other form.

The largest extractive industry in the area works the massive deposits of limestone which forms the scenery of about one-third of the

Park. About 95% of the limestone outcrop lies within the Park but it is the remaining 5% which contains most of the quarries The Park boundary was drawn so as to exclude these main quarrying areas near Buxton, Wirksworth and Cauldon Low. The limestone is in many places composed of almost 100% calcium carbonate; this makes it valuable in the chemical and steel industries. The range of goods in which limestone plays an important part in the production cycle is almost infinite; it includes the purification of gas and oil, the refining of sugar, paper making and the manufacture of glass, detergents and medicines. In steel manufacture the limestone is used to remove impurities. The other major use of limestone is as aggregate in the construction industry—for roadstone and concrete. Output of aggregate has increased eightfold since 1951, whereas the volume of material used in the chemical and steel industries has only doubled over the same period.

Cement manufacture is another important use. The Hope Cement works uses limestone and shale from the Hope Valley where the two geological types meet. The original major use for limestone—in agriculture—now accounts for about half of 1% of total output.

As the 5% of limestone outcrop outside the Park becomes worked out, increasing use is being made of the 95% within the boundary. In 1951, 0.8 million tons was produced within the Park, today that figure is 5.4 million tons—a sevenfold increase. On the other hand, outside the Park the 1951 figure was 4.9 million tons, it is now almost 12 million tons—only just over a doubling of production.

Despite these large increases in production the number of men employed in the limestone industry has declined. About 6,000 were employed directly in quarrying in 1951 (i.e. as quarrymen or in transport, etc.). This has now shrunk to below 4,000. The reason for this is that the industry has been transformed into a highly mechanised and automated operation.

Gritstone is the underlying rock of most of the remainder of the Park, This was formerly worked in many locations for building stone and millstones (hence the name Millstone Grit). This industry has also contracted greatly, but grindstones are still being exported to many parts of the world and there is still a specialised demand for building stone. Some quarries outside the Park work gritstone as a general-purpose aggregate.

In manufacturing industry there are many small units producing a wide variety of goods. The manufacture of textiles was the original industry of this type and the Peak District was in fact one of the birthplaces of the Industrial Revolution. Arkwright's first mill to use power was built at Cromford just outside the Park in 1770. Following the success of this operation other textile mills were built by Arkwright and others at Calver, Bakewell, Cressbrook, Edale and Bamford. Similar operations were established all around the northern and western boundaries of the Park, e.g. at Holmfirth, Hayfield, Glossop and Marple. Of all the mills in the Park only Litton Mill continues as a textile mill.

The others have many different new uses; for example, Calver now produces stainless steel sinks, Edale has been converted to flats.

Before the textile mills, corn mills and cheese factories were features of many villages. Since that time transport has become easier and the Peak District no longer has to be self-sufficient in agricultural produce. The area is now given wholly to dairying and livestock rearing, relying on direct transport of its products to the cities for processing. Of all these operations, the only cheese factory remaining is the one at Hartington, although butter is made at Leek and Nestlés have a factory at Ashbourne, both just outside the Park.

Other local industries include electronics components at Castleton, footwear at Eyam, and various factories associated with the Sheffield steel industry at Bakewell and the Hope Valley.

The location of the Park in the centre of industrial England can be seen to have been critical in its historical development, and is still vital to its economy. Water catchment for the cities developed during the 19th century and there are now 55 reservoirs in the Park. The result has been many changes to the upland economy as farmsteads and even small settlements disappeared. A third of the Park is used as gathering grounds and there is pressure to develop still more of the water resources. Many of the gathering grounds have subsidiary uses as grouse moors, for forestry, sheep grazing and for walking.

The outstanding scenic quality of the Park has been the latest of the area's resources to be utilised by the cities. Developing steadily since the start of the century and gathering pace since the second world war has been the use of the area for recreation. Something like 12 million visitor trips are made to the Park every year now, bringing benefit to the local economy as well as enjoyment to the townsman. It is for this combination of high scenic quality and recreation potential that the National Park was designated to be conserved and developed. In it lies the key to the area's future development.

9

The Work of the Planning Board

by THEO. S. BURRELL

SEVENTEEN million people live within 50 miles of the Peak District. Thirty-nine out of 40 visitors come for the day and their most common activity is to "drive around". Within this radius there are 3,000,000 cars and on an average summer Sunday afternoon about 100,000 of them head for the Park. The number of cars has increased sixfold since the Board back in 1951 was given the job of conserving the National Park and "promoting its enjoyment by the public".

The scenery that is enjoyed remains attractive because of the husbandry of the people who live within the National Park. The job of combining conservation with recreation and combining that with a concern for local people falls to a Board of 33 members: 8 are councillors from Derbyshire, 2 each are from Staffordshire, Cheshire, South Yorkshire, West Yorkshire, and Greater Manchester, 4 are from district councils and 11 are appointed by the Secretary of State for the Environment because of their special National Park interest.

CONSERVATION AND RECREATION

The qualities and traditions of this National Park, described in this guide-book, could all too easily be destroyed by the pressure upon it. Conservation means careful management for visitor use and the Board therefore places a great deal of emphasis on taking positive measures, to anticipate problems rather than be overtaken by events.

The way that the Board combines conservation with the provision of facilities for visitors can be illustrated by a scheme at Tideswell Dale. Here was a derelict quarry; its attendant machinery was removed, spoil heaps were seeded, trees planted, a car park was fitted into the landscape and picnic tables were provided by the Board's forestry works section. Members of the public can now use clearly defined paths within the Board's land and there is a National Park trail. Little trace remains of the former eyesore. Pressure has been reduced on other farmland.

Between Ashbourne and Hartington a disused railway has become the Tissington Trail, a route for walkers, cyclists and pony trekkers. Where there were stations there are now car parks and places to picnic, and the signal box at Hartington has become a warden briefing centre. The trail was then linked with the previous Cromford and High Peak line and that became the High Peak Trail, extending outside the Park and linked with other projects in Derbyshire.

Between these trails and Bakewell and Buxton another experiment is being carried out. Rather than widen roads to suit all the traffic that happens to use them, the Board with Derbyshire (the highway authority) has been reviewing the function of these sometimes ancient routes, and in the years ahead will be adapting them to ensure there is a good network for walking, riding, cycling, as well as for those visiting the area by car. The environmental qualities of each road have determined which ones shall be used for each purpose. Heavy lorries will be banned from many roads in this area.

In 1970 the Board pioneered the first motorless zone in a National Park. In the late sixties there had been congestion in the Goyt Valley at peak holiday times—motorists who visited the area in search of peace and quiet found a scene that looked more like a car park. Now new car parks exist around the edge of the area and on summer Sundays there are minibus services within the valley.

In 1973 the Board started on Sunday afternoons a new bus service to serve the Tissington Trail, and the plan for years ahead is to extend a system of public transport so that an attractive alternative to the car is provided. A new venture in 1974 is the production of a timetable giving all public transport services in the National Park. The latter is obtainable from information centres in the Park or by post from the National Park offices (addresses at page 82).

The Board has information centres at Bakewell, Edale, Castleton and Buxton, and a mobile centre. Together they have about 300,000 visitors a year. As well as offering information on local events the centres try to explain the natural environment as a Park and generally create a better understanding of the countryside. A wide range of publications is produced by the Peak Park Planning Board. In 1972 the first National Park Study Centre was opened at Losehill Hall, Castleton. The centre offers a variety of courses for people of all ages, for specialised groups and for the public in general. Further particulars can be obtained from the Administrative Officer, Losehill Hall, Castleton, Sheffield, S30 2WB.

There are National Park camp sites at Edale and Hayfield, there is a caravan site owned by the Board and run by the Caravan Club at Losehill Hall, and the Board owns hostels at Crowden-in-Longdendale and at Hagg Farm near the Snake Pass. The former is run by the Youth Hostels Association but is also open to non-members. The Board has also provided car parks and lay-bys for motorists; about 100 new parking spaces are established each year.

Before the National Park was formed, access to much of the moorland to the north was fiercely opposed, but the many walkers from surrounding towns pressed for better access. Like most land in the National Park, the area is privately owned. At times the conflict became a bitter one. The problem was reconciled by access agreements which the Board negotiated with landowners, and these agreements now cover about 76 square miles of "open country", generally the gritstone moorland to the north of the National Park.

The warden service was originally developed to patrol access land, but it is increasingly being extended to other areas as well. The Head Warden lives at Edale and there are 10 briefing centres from which warden patrols are organised.

Small woodlands are an important part of the scenery of the National Park and the Board now manages 70 of them, totalling some 600 acres. Groups of trees are felled and parts of a wood under-planted, a process which may be repeated four or five times over a period of 30 to 40 years, by which time about 60-70% of a woodland will have been replaced. Such woodlands are therefore likely to be still a fine landscape feature in a further 100 years' time. The Board's forestry works section plants about 50,000 new trees each year.

In 1966 the Board was awarded a diploma for conservation work by the Council of Europe. This was renewed for a further five years in 1971.

THE COST

75% grant is given towards most National Park work by national government. The remainder is precepted on the constituent authorities, who together have a rateable value of around £360 million. The Board's budget in 1973-4 was around £450,000.

THE FUTURE

Since 1951 not only has the number of cars in the area increased sixfold; the same is true within the National Park of the output of limestone. These two statistics illustrate two kinds of pressure now (in 1974) found in the Park. The first is a pressure that somehow must be faced—how to provide for the many visitors who come to enjoy the National Park. The second is an example of the kind of pressure increasingly difficult to reconcile with the job of managing a National Park. Other examples are through traffic and a demand for reservoirs. There are 55 reservoirs in the National Park already and there is a prospect of water demands doubling in the next 30 years. The moral which the Board draws from this is the need to find other methods of supply and to see if economies could be made.

Heavy through traffic is a good example of a problem not relevant to the idea of a Park. Yet the Peak District is ringed by cities which generate an increasing amount of heavy goods traffic on National Park roads. The Board is anxious to route such traffic on to a system of peripheral motorways and trunk routes as a means of preserving the landscape character and the qualities of peace and quiet which it was envisaged National Parks should have. It considers high priority should be given to a national strategy which faces the problem of inter-city movements,

PLATES XIX AND XX. Town houses of gritstone, in Castle Street, Bakewell; and (below) the Dower House at Hassop, now the post office, with limestone walls, gritstone dressings, and gritstone 'grey' slate roof

PLATE XXI. Farmyard and barn on the limestone plateau

PLATE XXII. Sheep shearing in the Edale Valley

PLATES XXIII AND XXIV. Car Park (above) and Picnic Site at Tideswell Dale provided by the Peak Park Planning Board

PLATES XXV AND XXVI.
Gritstone formations: Hen
Cloud (above); and
Stanage Edge, a classic
climbing ground

while respecting the National Park whose environment is so easily impaired.

As far as recreational traffic is concerned, in the years ahead the Board is likely to try to find new ways of providing for the enjoyment of scenery without destroying it in the process. Work on the Goyt Experiment and on improving systems of public transport is of great importance and, as the years go by, the authority is likely to seek new methods of management of the whole National Park.

The recent declaration of Lathkill Dale as a National Nature Reserve is perhaps an interesting first step towards effective zoning. Zoning ideas were developed further in a book published by the Board under the title *What Future for the Peak National Park?* An important part of the message was that in a National Park it is the quality of the environment which should determine how it is used.

10

Some Places of Interest

ALLGREAVE. This hamlet is at the southern end of the Wildboarclough Valley, where it is crossed by the Congleton-Buxton road. It is a good starting point for exploring the fine valleys forming the tributaries of the river Dane.

ALPORT. (a) A village on the Lathkill, 1 m. east of Youlgreave. Several 17th-century houses here, notably Monk's Hall. 1 m. south on Harthill Moor is a Bronze Age stone circle, with a small Iron Age earthwork, Castle Ring.

(b) A river, tributary of the Ashop, and rising on Bleaklow. Hence Alport Castles, a rocky edge on the east side of the valley. In the Alport Valley is a barn where the Woodlands Love Feast was celebrated on the first Sunday in July. This gathering of Nonconformists began in 1662, when under the Act of Uniformity three clergymen were ejected from their livings in Derby.

ALSTONFIELD. A village on the high ground between Dovedale and the Manifold. It, rather than Hartington, was the home village of Charles Cotton, Izaak Walton's friend and collaborator, and his carved pew is still in the church, which was built at intervals from Norman to Elizabethan times. There is a Saxon cross. The manor house bears the date 1587.

ARBOR LOW. The principal prehistoric monument of the Peak; 1 m. east of Parsley Hay.

ASHBOURNE. A few miles beyond the Park's southern border; a market town and important agricultural centre. It has a long history; and had a church at the time of Domesday Book. The present one, called by George Eliot 'the finest mere parish church in England', was rededicated in 1241, and part of the structure is of that date; the spire (212 feet high) is 14th century. Monuments of the Cockayne family run all but continuously from 1372 to 1592; a child, Penelope Boothby, dying at five, is commemorated in a touching marble figure by Thomas Banks. The grammar school was founded in 1585, and the old school is still used as a boys' boarding house. Opposite is the house of Dr. Johnson's friend, Dr. Taylor, where the Headmaster now lives. Almshouses still standing here were founded in 1640, 1669 and 1710. Johnson and Boswell stayed several times at the Green Man Hotel. There is a Saxon cross shaft in the church. Shrovetide football is played with hundreds a side on Shrove Tuesday and Ash Wednesday in and about Henmore Brook. Local industry includes a coffee-making plant and a corset works. Ashbourne Show is a big annual event.

ASHFORD-IN-THE-WATER. On the Wye, 1½ m. north of Bakewell, has three old bridges, of which the narrow Sheepwash Bridge abutting on to the A 6 is best known. Derbyshire 'black marble' used to be worked here.

AXE EDGE. (1,810 feet) 3 m. south-west of Buxton, is the highest point on the moorlands from which flow the rivers Dove, Manifold, Wye, Dane and Goyt.

BAKEWELL. Is the biggest place (pop. about 4,000) actually in the Peak District National Park, for Buxton lies in the industrialized enclave left out of it: and also one of the oldest. Bakewell was a place of consequence in Saxon days (as Baddecan Well): a Saxon cross stands in the churchyard, and the earthwork on Castle Hill may be that known to have been erected by Edward the Elder in 924. The church has Norman elements in it, but the main building is 13th to 14th century: the spire was rebuilt in 1852. The bridge over the Wye was built about 1300 (widened in the 19th century). The Market Hall was built in the late 17th century. Holme Hall (built 1626) is one of the most charming manor houses in the Peak. The grammar school was founded by Lady Manners in 1637, but now occupies a 20th-century building. At the Rutland Arms hotel (built 1804) the Bakewell pudding was first made (by mistake—an egg mixture meant for the pastry of a jam tart was poured into the jam). There is an important cattle market, and Bakewell Show is one of the biggest one-day shows in the country. The offices of the Peak Park Planning Board are at Aldern House, Baslow Road, and the National Park information centre is in the former Market Hall in the town centre.

BAMFORD. A large gritstone village in the Derwent Valley. It is the administrative centre for the three great reservoirs of the upper Derwent.

BASLOW. A characteristic gritstone village on the Derwent at the north entrance to Chatsworth Park. There is an old narrow humped bridge, and a more modern one. The part called Nether End is built round a triangular Goose Green.

BEELEY. At the southern entrance to Chatsworth. Beeley Hall is early 17th century, and Charles Dickens used to stay there.

BIRCHOVER. A hamlet 1 m. north of Winster, the centre of a group of gritstone crags, and also of prehistoric remains. The crags are Robin Hood's Stride, a narrow ridge with two pinnacles, Cratcliff Tor, the most cleancut of gritstone faces, and Rowtor Rocks, a pile of massive blocks. On Stanton Moor, to the east of Birchover are numerous barrows of the Middle Bronze Age, and two stone circles, the Nine Ladies and the Doll Tor. Another circle, the Nine Stones, is on Harthill Moor, a few miles away.

Birchover was the home of J. Clee Heathcote, a leading Derby-shire archaeologist. Antiquities discovered here by himself and his son are to be seen at the private museum owned by Mr. J. P. Heathcote. Birchover is mentioned in Domesday Book.

BLEAKLOW. The second highest hill in the Peak, lying between the Woodlands and Longdendale Valleys. Its highest point, Bleaklow Head, is about 2,061 feet above sea-level. The Pennine Way passes over it. Bleaklow is probably harder going than any hill in the Peak, even Kinder Scout.

BRADWELL. 2 m. south-east of Castleton; once a centre for lead mining, now for limestone quarrying, the lime being used mainly for cement making. There is a well-known cavern, Bagshaw's.

BROUGH. ½ m. south of Hope; site of Navio, a Roman military station.

BUXTON. The main town of the Peak, and a leading holiday resort and spa. It is just outside the National Park boundary. The medical virtues of its naturally tepid springs were recognized by the Romans, and attracted visitors for centuries after them. In 1780 the fifth Duke of Devonshire had the Crescent (meant to recall the Royal Crescent at Bath) built by John Carr of York, at a cost of £120,000, and the baths improved. Buxton is still a centre for the treatment of rheumatism and arthritis. There are a concert room and ballroom, a repertory theatre, two golf courses, a cricket ground where Derbyshire plays matches; and the Derby-shire croquet championships are held at Buxton.

BUXWORTH. (Formerly Bugsworth) 1 m. west of Chinley, the old terminus of the Peak Forest Canal, whence a tramway (the course is still visible) led up by Barmoor Clough to the lime quarries at Dove Holes. The tramway was made in 1795, and thirty horses were needed to keep it going. The now overgrown basin of the canal port is still there; its effective terminus is now at Whaley Bridge.

CALVER. A village on the Derwent, with an early cotton-spinning mill (1785) and 18th-century bridge, and a Methodist training centre, Cliff College.

CASTLETON. Capital of the Peak under the Norman kings, known for its castle and its caverns. The castle was first built in the 11th century by William Peveril, appointed bailiff to the royal manors in north-west Derbyshire by William I. The conspicuous keep was built by Henry II in 1176, as was the north-east gateway. The church dates in part from about 1200. The keep has been adopted as the emblem of the Peak Park Planning Board. The main caverns to be seen are the Peak Cavern (under Peveril Castle), the Blue John Cavern, the Speedwell Mine, and the Treak Cliff Cavern. Apart from the show caverns, Castleton is the potholing centre for the Peak. The restoration of Charles II is celebrated on 29 May by morris dancing, and the carrying round of a large garland of flowers by a man dressed as King Charles. The old road from the west reaches Castleton through a striking limestone gorge, the Winnats Pass.

CAT AND FIDDLE. An inn on the Buxton-Macclesfield road; second highest in England at 1,690 feet. (Tan Hill, in the Yorkshire Pennines, is 1,727 feet.)

CHAPEL-EN-LE-FRITH. Is just outside the Park boundary in the north-western enclave. The church (dedicated to St. Thomas à Becket) is partly 14th century, but much modified. (The original chapel, built in 1225 by the keepers of the Forest-Frith-of the Peak has wholly disappeared.) There is a big factory making brake linings for cars, and also industrial beltings and abrasives.

1 m. north-east of Chapel is Ford Hall, for 300 years the home of the Bagshawe family. Its most notable member, William Bagshawe, nonconformist 'Apostle of the Peak', was one of the clergy who lost his living at Glossop as a result of the Act of Uniformity in 1662. 1 m. west of Chapel is Bradshaw Hall, now a farm, and formerly the home of the Bradshaw family, of whom the most eminent was John Bradshaw of Marple, president of the court which tried King Charles I and condemned him to execution.

CHATSWORTH. The seat of the Duke of Devonshire, and the most visited of all the 'great houses' of the Peak (and about third in Great Britain), for its collection of works of art, its architecture, and its gardens, laid out by Sir Joseph Paxton. It is open to the public, but check times locally.

CHELMORTON. 5 m. south-east of Buxton. The church (one of the highest placed in the country, at 1,200 feet) is partly 13th-century work.

CHINLEY. Has a railway station on the line from Sheffield through Edale. A popular starting point for walkers.

CROWDEN-IN-LONGDENDALE. A hamlet in the Longdendale Valley, north of Bleaklow. The National Park Youth Hostel is situated there.

DANE. The chief river of the south-west moors. It rises close to Axe Edge, passes in a deep bare valley past Three Shires Head (Derbyshire, Cheshire and Staffordshire), then through a beautifully wooded valley past Danebridge, and out into the Cheshire Plain near Rushton Spencer.

DERWENT. The chief river of the Peak, rising near Bleaklow, and flowing south past Hathersage, Chatsworth, Great Rowsley and Matlock. Its head waters feed the three large reservoirs of the Derwent Valley Water Board, Howden, Derwent and Ladybower. The third submerged the villages of Ashopton and Derwent Woodlands, Derwent Hall (built 1672) and the old pack bridge, which was in 1959 rebuilt higher up the river, near Slippery Stones. Below the reservoirs the valley is well wooded and well populated.

DOCTOR'S GATE. The highest part of the Roman road from Melandra (Glossop) to Navio (Brough).

DOVEDALE. The most famous of the limestone valleys. The Dove has really four sections. The uppermost flows through a fairly broad valley with limestone hills on the east and shale or gritstone on the west. In the second section below Hartington the river becomes narrow, known first as Beresford Dale, then as Wolfscote Dale. There is a brief break at Milldale, then another stretch of three to four miles, commonly called 'Dovedale' without qualification. This has wonderful limestone crags and lush vegetation, and belongs to the National Trust. The river is famous for trout. The fourth section, below Thorpe Cloud, is broad and open again, and outside the National Park.

ECTON. Ecton coppermine, in the Manifold Valley, was worked in the 17th and 18th centuries. The fifth Duke of Devonshire is said to have applied its profits to the building of the Crescent at Buxton. It has long been unworked; only its spoil heap remains to scar the valley; it is now being planted over.

EDALE. Immediately south of Kinder Scout, is probably the most popular walking centre in the Peak. There is also ski-ing in winter. The Peak Board's warden service is based in Edale, where there are also a National Park information centre, and a mountain rescue post. The southern end of the Pennine Way is at Edale.

EDENSOR. Is the satellite village of Chatsworth, and is at the east entrance to the Park. It was rebuilt on this site in 1839, in a fanciful style, to be out of sight of the hall, but the village institute, formerly an inn, is Georgian.

ELDON HILL. 3 m. south-west from Castleton, is the highest (1,548 feet) of the limestone hills of the Peak. Its north-western face is quarried. On its southern slope is Eldon Hole, the Peak's one conspicuous pothole, once believed to be bottomless, but actually 186 feet deep.

ELTON. 1 m. west of Winster, an old lead-mining village. The hall is now a youth hostel.

EYAM. An ancient and famous village on the limestone shelf north of Middleton Dale. There is a carved Saxon cross in the churchyard; the church has a 13th-century chancel and a Norman font. Eyam Hall is dated 1676, the rectory is mid-Georgian. Eyam suffered tragically from the Great Plague of 1665, the infection being carried, it is believed, in a box of clothes from London.

The rector, William Mompesson, persuaded the people to stay and face the risk of death rather than flee and spread the infection; about five out of six died. To avoid assembling in church, the people worshipped at 'Cucklett Church', a limestone bluff in a little valley called 'The Delf'. A Barmote (the medieval court for settling disputes in lead mining) still meets periodically at Eyam. The Glebe mine produces much fluorspar and some lead: and shoes are made here.

On Wet Withens moor, 2 m. north-north-east of Eyam, is a Bronze Age stone circle.

FENNY BENTLEY. An attractive village about 2 m. north of Ashbourne. The church has an interesting interior.

FLAGG. On the plateau south of Taddington Moor, has a 16th-century hall. The High Peak Hunt's point-to-point races are held on Flagg Moor.

FLASH. Claims to be the highest village in England (at 1,518 feet). It is 5 m. south-west of Buxton, and almost on the Derbyshire-Staffordshire border. The Traveller's Rest at Flash Bar (1,535 feet) is one of the half-dozen 'highest inns'.

FRIDEN. 2 m. east of Hartington, has an important secondary industry; it makes refractory bricks from the silica sand found in the neighbourhood in deep isolated pockets.

GLOSSOP. A town of 19,000 people just outside the Park boundary on the north-west, and the starting point for the Snake Road, and Doctor's Gate.

GOYT. This river is a tributary of the Mersey, rising near Axe Edge and running north to join the Etherow from Longdendale at Marple. The valley is richly wooded, and contains one of Stockport's reservoirs.

GRINDLEFORD. The first railway station on the Peak side of the Dore tunnel, through which the Sheffield-Chinley railway enters the Park. Padley chapel, formerly attached to the manor house (built 15th century) is remembered for the arrest in 1588 of two Roman Catholic priests, later executed at Derby: their memory is honoured by an annual pilgrimage. A mile above Grindleford is Longshaw Lodge, once a shooting box, now owned by the National Trust, and the scene of annual sheep-dog trials, held on the first Thursday in September.

HADDON HALL. This beautiful medieval 'great house', with Elizabethan and Jacobean additions, 2 miles south of Bakewell, belongs to the Duke of Rutland. It is open to the public, but check times locally.

HARTINGTON. A small market town just off the Dove, a good fishing centre. The church is 13th- and 14th-century work; Hartington Hall, built in 1611, is now a youth hostel. In the Charles Cotton Hotel are drawings and verses by Cotton, 17th-century poet and fisherman, who introduced Izaak Walton to the Peak, and wrote the second part of the 'Compleat Angler'. In Beresford Dale, about 1 m. south, is a small square fishing house, built by Cotton in 1674 as a memento of his fishing days with 'my father Walton'.

HASSOP. 3 m. north of Bakewell, has a mainly Jacobean hall, formerly and for long the home of the Eyres, a leading Roman Catholic family: a Catholic church (1816) in the classical revival style, and a fine avenue of trees.

HATHERSAGE. The main village of the middle Derwent Valley. The church was built in 1381, but much altered: in the churchyard is a very large grave, by tradition that of Little John, of Robin Hood's company. Notable brasses of the Eyre family are in the church. Carl Wark, 2 m. east, is a prehistoric stone fort, and Camp Green is a fine castle mound, probably Norman. Moorseats ½ m. north-east is probably the house described as Moor House in Charlotte Brontë's 'Jane Eyre'. Charlotte stayed in Hathersage with her friend Ellen Nussey, whose brother was vicar there. Other interesting houses are Hazelford, 1 m. south (17th century) and Highlow Hall, 1½ m. south-west (probably 16th century), and North Lees Hall, probably the 'Thornfield Hall' of 'Jane Eyre'.

HAYFIELD. An industrial village (cotton, paper), on the river Sett, below the west face of Kinder Scout, which is commonly climbed from it. The song 'Come lasses and lads' is said to have been written with reference to its fair.

HOLME MOSS. A moorland height just off the Greenfield-Holmfirth road. It carries a B.B.C. radio and T.V. transmitter, the mast of which is visible from a great distance.

HOPE. A substantial and ancient village in the broad valley of the Noe, 1½ m. east of Castleton. The church has an early 14th-century tower with a spire, but has been much modified. Among monuments inside are two 13th-century slabs commemorating officials of the Peak Forest. A Saxon cross stands near the church.

HUCKLOW, GREAT. 2 m. north of Tideswell, well known for its village drama centre. An old barn has been fitted up as a theatre, and plays are given on several weeks a year—when the moon is full, to facilitate walking home. The moving spirit was Dr. L. du Garde Peach.

ILAM. A village at the foot of the Manifold Valley 1 m. above the junction of the Manifold with the Dove. Ilam Hall, rebuilt in the 19th century, is now a youth hostel, and there is a Saxon cross shaft in the grounds. The Izaak Walton Hotel is a classic house for trout fishermen. Much of the church was rebuilt in the 19th century, but there are two Saxon crosses built into its walls and two in the churchyard.

JENKIN CHAPEL. A very simple chapel of St. John, built about 1700, near the head of the Todd Brook. It stands by the old salt trade route from Cheshire into Derbyshire: Saltersford Hall, a 16th-century farmhouse, is ¼ mile south.

KETTLESHULME. A village in the valley of the Todd Brook, a tributary of the Goyt; has a youth hostel lying beneath Windgather Rocks, a gritstone outcrop much used for teaching beginners to climb.

KINDER SCOUT. The highest hill area in the Peak, rising to 2,088 feet. The summit is a long triangular plateau, mainly covered with peat bog: the sides are steep, and sometimes precipitous. The river Kinder, rising near the highest point, flows over the Downfall on the western escarpment; deep channels are cut into the flanks of the hill by the Fair Brook and Blackden Brook on the north, Grinds Brook and Crowden Brook on the south, and Jagger's Clough on the east. There is good gritstone climbing on many of the edges. Kinder Scout is a favourite mountain with strong walkers, and the first to which the access provisions of the National Parks Act were successfully applied.

LANGSETT. On the Yorkshire border of the Park; a starting point for the Cut Gate pass into the Derwent Valley.

LONGDENDALE. The valley of the Etherow, one of the three streams which compose the Mersey. It holds an ancient road from Cheshire into Yorkshire by Salter's Brook Bridge, the electrified railway line between Manchester and Sheffield, and five Manchester reservoirs.

LONGNOR. In the north-east corner of Staffordshire, between the Dove and the Manifold, it holds an annual sports day, with racing on foot, on horseback and on motor-cycle. In the church is a memorial to William Bellinge, who is said to have lived to 112, and fought in the battle of Ramillies.

LONGSTONE, GREAT. 2½ m. north of Bakewell, has one long street. A fine avenue of elms links the village green with the hall, built in 1747. The church dates from the 13th century and was carefully restored by Norman Shaw in 1873. Longstone Head commands a superb view of the Wye and Monsal Dale.

LYME HALL. Is the third 'great house' of the Peak, though a long way after Chatsworth and Haddon in fame. It lies in the north-west corner of the Park, overlooking Stockport. Lyme Hall and Lyme Park now belong to the National Trust, but are leased to Stockport Corporation.
There are Tudor and Jacobean rooms in the hall, but it was partly rebuilt by Leoni in the 18th century. The Legh family lived here from the 14th century until 1947. A herd of red deer is still maintained.

MAM TOR. A conspicuous hill (1,696 feet) on the south side of the Edale Valley. It is composed of a rather unstable sandstone and shales, and the south face, a slowly disintegrating cliff, has given it the name of 'The Shivering Mountain'. Earthworks of the Iron Age enclose sixteen acres of the summit. A fine narrow ridge runs north-east for three miles from Mam Tor to Lose Hill.

MANIFOLD. This river is the companion stream to the Dove. They rise within a mile of each other on Axe Edge, flow roughly parallel for 20 miles, and join when they both emerge from their limestone gorges. The Manifold Valley begins broad and open, like the upper Dove. It becomes narrow and rocky after Hulme End. At Thor's Cave relics of occupation by early man have been found. At Beeston Tor, another gorge, that of the river Hamps, comes in from the south-west. In this reach the Manifold runs underground in dry weather, reappearing in the grounds of Ilam Hall. A light railway used to run from Hulme End to Beeston Tor, and then through the Hamps gorge to Waterhouses. Abandoned as a railway, it was converted into a tarmacadam path, wide enough for one car, but not open to through traffic, except from the farms of the valley, and to a limited extent from Redhurst Halt to Butterton station.

MATLOCK. Matlock and Matlock Bath, just outside the Park to the south, are important holiday resorts. The High Tor, a 400-foot limestone crag, towers over the valley between the two. Smedley's Hydro, very popular when medical treatment by 'the waters' was fashionable, is now the offices of the Derbyshire County Council. There are thermal waters at Matlock Bath; show caverns and fine walks add to the attractions.

MILLER'S DALE. A section of the Wye Valley between Chee Dale and Monsal Dale. Chee Tor, 1 m. up the river from the former station, is probably the finest single limestone crag in the Park. Two miles down the valley is Litton Mill, an early cotton mill, still working (but nylon now, not cotton). Above the dale on the north side is Ravenstor youth hostel.

MONYASH. On the limestone plateau south of Flagg, was once a market town and a lead-mining centre for the High Peak. The church was founded in 1198, and contains a great iron-bound oak parish chest, perhaps dating from the 13th century. John Gratton, an early Quaker, was born here in 1640. The tradition he founded lasted more than two centuries. John Bright (who was descended from Gratton on his mother's side) often stayed with a Quaker family, the Bowmans, at One Ash farm—originally a penitentiary for disobedient monks from Roche Abbey in Yorkshire.

PEAK FOREST. Was originally the name of a royal forest (in the legal sense). The present village is near the middle, and may have served as an administrative or religious centre at one time. The church here was for centuries extra-parochial, and came under no bishop; the incumbent could grant licences for marriage and prove wills. It became a favourite place for run-away marriages, which at one time were as many as sixty a year, and were entered on the register as 'foreign marriages'. (The practice ended in 1804, but this marrying of 'foreigners' was revived in 1938, with the condition that one partner must have lived at Peak Forest for fifteen days before the marriage.) The church is of King Charles the Martyr—a rare dedication.

ROWARTH. A hamlet in a broad valley 3 m. north of New Mills. Among its buildings is Long Lee farm, built in 1663 (but in the Tudor tradition), and the Little Mill Inn, built 1781. There are some handsome gritstone farm houses on the higher slopes—Back Rowarth, Upper Rowarth, and Ringstones.

ROWSLEY. At the junction of the Derwent and the Wye, it was for twenty years the northward railhead of the line from the south, now extended through Miller's Dale to Chinley. There is a famous hotel, the Peacock, built in 1652.

STANTON-IN-THE-PEAK. Stands at the north end of Stanton Moor. Stanton Hall (part 17th, part 18th century) has a park of 130 acres and a herd of deer. Stanton Old Hall was built in 1667, and is now a farm.

STONEY MIDDLETON. Is at the foot of Middleton Dale, the valley in the Peak most quarried (for limestone). The houses are built in tiers on the sides of the valley. There is a curious octagonal church added in 1759 to an earlier tower. The hall is of Elizabethan date. There is a substantial boot-making industry here.

TADDINGTON MOOR. The highest point of the limestone hills south of the Wye, as Eldon Hill is north of it; the summit (known as Sough Top) falls just short of 1,500 feet. There is near the top a fine chambered Neolithic barrow, Five Wells tumulus. Taddington village is north-east of the moor and 400 feet lower. The church has a 14th-century tower.

TIDESWELL. Has a masterly air about it, from its wide street and its great church. Unlike most of those in the Peak this was built almost all in one period (the 14th century), but a period in which the style was developing from the Decorated to the Perpendicular manner over the 75 years or so that the church was building. Thus the beautifully flowing tracery of the transept and east windows is typically Decorated, the west tower wholly Perpendicular; the striking straight-headed windows of the chancel are intermediate, and strive towards the Perpendicular spirit. The church is rich in brasses and other monuments. The brass memorial to John Foljambe is the earliest in Derbyshire

(1383); there is another to Pursglove, Bishop of Hull, who founded a grammar school in Tideswell (1578); and another to Sampson Meverill, Knight Constable of England (1462), who fought against Joan of Arc in the Hundred Years War. Tideswell was granted a market charter in 1250. It is in a small way a manufacturing centre, making plastics and magnets. At Litton, 1 m. east, is a charming green with grey limestone houses round it. Wheston, 1 m. west, has a 15th-century village cross.

TISSINGTON. The neatest village in the Peak, with grey stone houses on two sides of a triangular green, and the church on the third. The church has a Norman tower and south doorway, with some pseudo-Norman additions. The hall is Jacobean, and long the home of the Fitzherbert family. Tissington is also the original home of the custom of well dressing on Ascension Day each year (decorating wells and springs with pictures or designs made of flowers pressed into wet clay), which is now practised in many other places in the Peak.

WATERHOUSES. Lies on the Ashbourne-Leek road on the border of the Park; it was formerly the terminus of the Manifold Valley Railway and so has become the starting point of the footpath which replaced the line.

WETTON. A moorland village on the high ground between the Dove and the Manifold gorges. Close to Wetton is Long Low, an extraordinary prehistoric monument.

WILDBOARCLOUGH. A small village in the bottom of the steep-sided valley of the same name. Part of the old mill survives as a post office and the 'Edwardian' church is interesting. The nearest settlement to the pyramid peak of Shutlings Low.

WINCLE (and DANEBRIDGE). A scattered village near to the wooded gorge of the river Dane, below the confluence of several tributaries. Here is the meeting place between the richer countryside of the plain and the severe scenery of the National Park hills.

WINSTER. An ancient lead-mining town, with many handsome houses, and a market hall (now owned by the National Trust), with stone arches (filled in) on the ground floor, and an upper storey of brick; the latter built in the 17th century, the former perhaps in the 15th. It is a great place for morris dancing.

WORMHILL. 1 m. north-west of Miller's Dale, has a hall built in 1697, and an earlier Old Hall farm. But it is more notable as the birthplace of James Brindley, the almost illiterate engineer, who astonished the 18th century by building the Bridgwater and many other canals. The cottage where he was born has disappeared.

YOULGREAVE. A big village between the Lathkill and Bradford rivers. The church has a noble 15th-century tower, a mainly Norman body, and a great variety of monuments within. There is a unique double font (dated about 1200), and an east window by William Morris and Edward Burne-Jones. Well dressing has been practised at Youlgreave for much longer than at most other places, though not as long as at Tissington. 1 m. west of Youlgreave is Lomberdale Hall, the home of Thomas Bateman, the Derbyshire antiquarian. His tomb, surmounted by a stone model of a Bronze Age urn, is ½ m. further, behind the Congregational church at Middleton.

II

Sport in the Peak

MANY people who come to the Peak for recreation come to walk, or for the allied pastimes appropriate to hill country—rock climbing, potholing and occasionally ski-ing.

For those who take their walking seriously the high moorlands in the northern part of the Park—Kinder Scout, Bleaklow, Black Hill, Derwent Edge—are attractive in all weathers. The going is hard; tracks are relatively few; physical fitness and skill in map-and-compass work are essential. So are proper clothes, especially in winter or in bad weather at any season—strong boots, long woollen socks, long trousers or breeches (but not jeans), an anorak or wind-proof jacket, and a rucksack to carry spare clothing, waterproofs and food. Besides a map (the 1-inch Ordnance Survey, or the 2½-inch Ordnance Survey Dark Peak map) and compass, it is wise to carry a whistle and a torch in case of being benighted or of injury to one of the party. The Mountain Rescue Committee produces an inexpensive booklet annually giving details of mountain rescue facilities; this is available by post from the Board's offices, or by calling personally at National Park information centres. Serious mishaps are rare, but they do happen, and the volunteers involved in mountain rescue work are concerned at the number of minor calls to assist those who underestimate the difficulties of these moors, or fail to prepare for serious hill walking. Inexpert walkers would be well advised to leave these moors alone unless they have experienced companions with them. The Peak District section of the Pennine Way, which starts at Edale, goes almost entirely over country of this kind; the first two days in particular are long and give strenuous walking. Those setting out on the Way should ensure they are in training for hard walking and have emergency equipment, but are not carrying too heavy a load.

The Peak Board has negotiated access agreements with the landowners of many of the most popular moorlands. Agreements now give the public the privilege of wandering over the famous Kinder and Bleaklow plateaux, the Chew, Longdendale and Langsett Moors, and Stanage and most of the eastern gritstone edges, subject to the observance of the bye-laws for behaviour on access land (which incorporate the Country Code). These agreements include clauses whereby public access is withdrawn for a few days each year for grouse shooting, between 12 August and 10 December (rarely after October); daily notices are displayed around each moor when access is withdrawn and monthly closure lists are available from the Board's offices—please send a stamped addressed envelope. Camping is not allowed without the landowner's consent, nor are Service training, organised games, competitions or sponsored walks; and dogs must be on leads.

There is *no public right of access* to the enclosures below this open moorland except on footpaths. The Board established a warden service as soon as its first access agreements were completed. The main objects of this service are to offer guidance and help to the public, and to protect their interests, and those of the landowners, by enforcing the bye-laws if necessary. Wardens can be identified by a yellow armband which they wear when patrolling access land or areas owned by the Board. Those interested in training to become wardens should write to the Peak National Park office.

The White Peak is more extensively farmed than the gritstone moors. This limestone part of the Peak National Park, with its well-known dales, is covered by an extensive network of footpaths and bridleways, some of which date from pre-Roman times. Accurate navigation ($2\frac{1}{2}$-inch maps) is also required here to avoid losing the way in a maze of small enclosures, the old dry limestone walls of which are particularly susceptible to damage by thoughtless walkers who have lost their way. Paths and tracks indicated on Ordnance Survey maps are not necessarily public rights of way; they are a representation of what appeared on the ground when the survey was carried out, although some of them may now have fallen into disuse. Although the White Peak is generally easy walking country, old mining shafts and caves are a particular danger.

The Peak is an important rock climbing area, with gritstone escarpments giving climbs from 30 to 100 feet, some of which are suitable for beginners while others are technically very hard, and limestone cliffs in dales, most of which are longer and of a very high standard.

There are many caves and potholes in the limestone country. Some of the caves (especially at and near Castleton) have been equipped with steps, lights, etc., for visitors. Many others, descended and explored by serious cavers, are technically difficult, and the inexperienced are advised to contact a local club. Permission should first be obtained from the owner or tenant. As with mountain rescue, the people who help with cave emergencies, co-ordinated by the Derbyshire Cave Rescue Organisation, are volunteers. Caves in the Peak District often have beautiful and unusual geological formations, and these should not be damaged as they are also important from a scientific point of view.

A ski-run of half a mile or so, in part on land owned by the Peak Board, draws enthusiasts to Edale; and there is a fair amount of ski-ing elsewhere when the snow serves, notably on the slopes falling from the Chapel-en-le-Frith to Castleton road, round Buxton, and near Holme Moss.

Those who like horse or pony riding will be able to enjoy many a quiet lane or bridleway in the Peak District, but generally the moorlands of the north are unsuitable.

Other organised pursuits include gliding—the Derbyshire and Lancashire Gliding Club has an important site on the edge above Great Hucklow.

Golfers will find courses at Bamford and Bakewell, and outside the Park at Buxton, Matlock and Ashbourne.

As for sport on or in the water, the Peak has some admirable fishing rivers, especially for trout and grayling. While the rights are largely owned by local angling clubs and not available for visitors, some stretches of water are controlled by hotels and open to those staying in them. There is some sailing under the auspices of local clubs, but inquiries should be made well in advance. The Peak's rivers are not much used for bathing but there are swimming pools in the Park, at Hathersage and Bamford, and just outside it at Matlock, Matlock Bath, Ashbourne and Buxton. Unfortunately there are few places where riparian interests will allow canoeing, and canoeing without permission on rivers long famed for fishing can only jeopardise any future negotiations for access to rivers.

Further information on the activities mentioned may be obtained from the national organisations concerned, listed in the Appendix, or failing this from the Board's offices. A selection of free information leaflets and a list of publications are available from the Board on receipt of a large stamped addressed envelope.

BIBLIOGRAPHY

THE PEAK DISTRICT

BAGSHAW, S. *History, Gazetteer, and Directory of Derbyshire.* 1846.
BATES, A. *Green tracks in Derbyshire: a guide to 32 walks.* 1961. Dalesman Publishing Co., Clapham, via Lancaster.
BELLHOUSE, Mrs. M. L. *Combs—My Village.*
BINNS, A. P. *Walking the Pennine Way.* Gerrard.
British Association. *Manchester and its region.* 1962. Manchester U.P.
British Association. *Sheffield and its region.* 1956.
Country Life. *Picture Book of the Peak District.* 1961. Country Life Ltd.
Derbyshire County Library. *Derbyshire: a list of books about the county.* 2nd ed. 1969.
The Derbyshire Guide (Annual). Derbyshire Countryside Ltd., Lodge Lane, Derby.
Derbyshire Life and Countryside (Monthly magazine). 1931-date. Derbyshire Countryside Ltd.
Derbyshire County Handbook. 4th ed., 1971. Derbyshire County Council.
DERRY, J. *Across the Derbyshire Moors.* 26th ed. by G. H. B. Ward, 1952. Sheffield Telegraph and Star Ltd.
DURY, G. H. *The East Midlands and the Peak (Regions of the British Isles series).* 1963. Nelson.
EDWARDS, K. C. *The Peak District (New Naturalist series).* 1962. Collins.
GLOVER, S. *The history and gazetteer of the County of Derby.* 2 vols., 1831.
HAWORTH, J., ed. *The Pennine Way and walks in Derbyshire.* 1967. Derbyshire Countryside Ltd.
HAWORTH, J., ed. *Walking in Derbyshire.* 4th rev. ed., 1972. Derbyshire Countryside Ltd.
INGRAM, J. H. *Companion into Cheshire.* 2nd ed., 1948.
The River Trent (includes Derwent, Dove, Wye, etc.). 1955. Cassell.
JEWITT, A. *The History of Buxton.* 1811.
KIRKHAM, N. *Derbyshire (Vision of England series).* 1947. Elek.
Little Guides series. GALLICHAN, W. M., *Cheshire,* 4th ed. by E. H. Mason, 1957; TUDOR, T., *Derbyshire,* 5th ed. by E. C. Williams, 1950; MASEFIELD, C. J. B., *Staffordshire,* 4th ed. by R. L. P. Jowitt, 1930. Methuen.
MANTELL, K. *Dovedale Guide.* New ed., 1960. Derbyshire Countryside Ltd.
MARRIOTT, M. *The Shell Book of the Pennine Way.* 1968.
MEE, A. *Cheshire,* 1968; *Derbyshire,* 1969; *Staffordshire,* 1971. Hodder and Stoughton.
MOUNTFORD, P. H., and MYERS, J. *North Staffordshire Landscape,* 1951. L. Orridge, Red Lion Square, Newcastle-under-Lyme.
OLDHAM, K. *The Pennine Way.* 2nd ed., 1968.
Peak Park Planning Board. Peak District National Park Development Plan: Report and Analysis of Survey; Park Maps, etc., 1955; Development Plan Review; Report and Analysis of Survey: 1966: Accommodation and Catering Guide, 1968. *Walks around . . . series (Edale Longdendale, Dovedale, Eyam and Hathersage). What Future for the Peak National Park?,* 1972. *The Peak—the Story of a National Park,* 1972.
PORTEOUS, C. *Peakland. (Regional Books series).* 1954. Hale.
PORTEOUS, C. *Portrait of Peakland.* 1963. Hale.
POUCHER, W. A. *The Peak and Pennines.* 1966. Constable.
RAISTRICK, A. *Pennine walls.* New ed., 1961. Dalesman Publishing Co., Clapham, via Lancaster.

71

RATHBONE, C. *Dane Valley Story.* 1953. Macclesfield Press Ltd.
RATHBONE, C. *Goyt Valley Story.* Macclesfield Press Ltd.
REDFERN, R. *Rambles in Peakland.* 1965. Hale.
SAINTER, J. D. *Rambles round Macclesfield.* 1878.
Sheffield Clarion Ramblers. Handbook. 1900-64.
WAINWRIGHT, A. *Pennine Way Companion; a pictorial guide.* 1968.
Ward Lock and Co. Ltd. *Guide to the Peak District.* 5th ed., 1965. Ward Lock.
WILLIAMS, E. C. *Companion into Derbyshire.* 2nd ed., 1950. Methuen.
WRIGHT, C. J. *A guide to the Pennine Way.* 1967.
Youth Hostels Association. *Youth Hostels in the Peak District.* New ed., 1966.
    Y.H.A. Peak Regional Group.

AGRICULTURE AND INDUSTRY

Derwent Valley Water Board. A short history of the undertaking. 1945. Bamford,
    Derbyshire.
EGGLESTONE, W. M. The occurrence and commercial uses of fluorspar.
    (*Instititution of Mining Engineers Transactions,* Vol. 35, 1907-08).
FAREY, J. M. *General view of the agriculture and minerals of Derbyshire.* 3 vols.,
    1811-17. Board of Agriculture.
FORD, T. D., and RIEUWERTS, J. H., eds. *Lead Mining in the Peak District.*
    Compiled by members of the Peak District Mines Historical Society, 1968.
    Peak Park Planning Board.
FUSSELL, G. E. Four centuries of farming systems in Derbyshire, 1500-1900.
    Derbyshire Archaeological Society Journal, Vol. 71).)
HARRIS, H. *Industrial Archaeology of the Peak District,* 1971. David & Charles.
HOLLAND, H. *General view of the agriculture of Cheshire.* 1808. Board of
    Agriculture.
KIRKHAM, N. *Derbyshire Lead Mining through the Centuries.* 1968. D. Bradford
    Barton Ltd.
Land Utilization Survey. The Land of Britain. Part 63: *Derbyshire,* by A. H.
    Harris, etc. 1941. London School of Economics, University of London.
'Manifold'. *The Leek and Manifold Light Railway.* New ed., 1965. Truro,
    Barton. *The North Staffordshire Railway.* 1952. Henstock.
MERCER, W. *The Agriculture of Cheshire.* Royal Agricultural Society of England.
NIXON, F. *The early steam engine in Derbyshire.* 1957. Newcomen Society.
NIXON, F. *Industrial Archaeology of Derbyshire.* 1969. David & Charles.
Nottingham University School of Agriculture. *The pattern of farming in the
    East Midlands,* by R. B. Jones. 1954.
Peak District Mines Historical Society, *Bulletin.*
PITT, W. *General view of the agriculture of the county of Stafford.* 2nd ed., 1813.
RAISTRICK, A., and JENNINGS, B. *A history of lead mining in the Pennines.* 1965.
    Longmans.
RIMMER, A. *The Cromford and High Peak Railway.* New ed., 1962. Oakwood
    Press, Lingfield, Surrey.
STOKES, A. H. Lead and lead mining in Derbyshire. (*Transactions of the
    Chesterfield and Derbyshire Institute of Mining Engineers,* Vols. 8, 9 and 11,
    1880-83). Reprinted in typescript by the Peak District Mines Historical
    Society, 1964.
STURGESS, R. W. Agricultural change in the Staffordshire moorlands, 1780-1850.
    (*North Staffordshire Journal of Field Studies,* Vol. 1). The University, Keele,
    Staffs.
TAPPING. W. *Treatise on the Derbyshire mining customs and Mineral Court Act,*
    1852. 1854. Shaw and Sons.
TUNMER, E. J. E. Blue John Working. (*Transactions of the Hunter Archaelogical
    Society,* Vol. 5, 1942). The Society, The University, Sheffield.

BUILDINGS

Chatsworth. Rev. ed. 1973. Derbyshire Countryside Ltd.
COX, J. C. *Notes on the churches of Derbyshire.* Vol. 2, *The High Peak.* 1877.
    Bemrose.

MANTELL, K. H. *Haddon Hall*. Rev. ed., 1966. English Life Publications, Derby.
Department of the Environment. *Peveril Castle, Derbyshire*, by B. H. St. J. O'Neil. 1950. H.M.S.O.
Peak Park Planning Board, *Building in the Peak*. Rev. ed., 1973.
PEVSNER, N. *Derbyshire (Buildings of England series)*. 1953. Penguin.
RICHARDS, R. *Old Cheshire churches*. 1947. Batsford.
SMITH, G. LE B. *Haddon*. 1906. Elliot Stock.
TARN, J. N. *The Peak National Park—its Architecture*. 1971.
THOMPSON, F. *Chatsworth; a short history*. 1951. Country Life. *A history of Chatsworth*. 1949. Country Life.

CLIMBING, CAVES AND CAVING

British Caving, *ed*. Cullingford. 1962. Routledge and Kegan Paul.
BYNE, E., and SUTTON, G. *High Peak; the story of walking and climbing in the Peak*. 1966. Secker and Warburg.
BYNE, E., *ed. Rock climbs in the Peak*. Vol. 1, The Sheffield-Stanage area. 1964. Vol. 2, The Saddleworth-Chew Valley area. 1965. Vol. 3, The Sheffield-Froggatt area. 1966. Cade. Other titles in preparation.
CULLINGFORD, *ed. Manual of caving techniques*. Routledge and Kegan Paul.
FORD, T. D., and others, *eds. The caves of Derbyshire*. Rev. ed., 1967. Dalesman Publishing Co., Clapham, via Lancaster.
Pennine Underground. 1963. Dalesman Publishing Co., Clapham, via Lancaster.

CUSTOMS, FOLKLORE

JEWITT, L. *Ballads and songs of Derbyshire*. 1867. Bemrose.
PEGGE, S. *Two collections of Derbicisms*. 1896. English Dialect Society.
PLATT, W. *Peakland humours*. 1926. Folk Press.
PORTEOUS, C. *The ancient customs of Derbyshire*. 1960. Derbyshire Countryside Ltd.
PORTEOUS, C. *The well-dressing guide*. Rev. ed., 1967. Derbyshire Countryside Ltd.
TURNER, W. *Romances of the Peak*. 1901. Simpkin Marshall.
WOOD, W. *Tales and traditions of the High Peak*. 1862. Bell and Daldy.

FROM THE EARLIEST TIMES

ARMITAGE, H. *Early man in Hallamshire*. 1939. Sampson Low.
BATEMAN, T. *Ten years' diggings in Celtic and Saxon grave hills*. 1861. Bemrose. *Vestiges of the antiquities of Derbyshire*. 1848. J. R. Smith, 4 Old Compton Street, London.
BULMER, T., and Co. *History, topography and directory of Derbyshire*. 1895.
BÚLOCK, J. D. The Bronze Age in the North-West. (*Transactions of the Lancashire and Cheshire Antiquarian Society*. Vol. 71).
BURTON, I. E., *ed. The Royal Forest of the Peak*. New ed., 1966. Peak Park Planning Board.
BUTTERWORTH, A., and LEWIS, D. G. *Prehistoric and Roman times in the Sheffield Area*. 2nd ed., 1972. Sheffield City Museum.
COX, J. C. *Memorials of old Derbyshire*. 1907. Bemrose.
DANIEL, C. A. *Peakland portfolio*. 1948. The Author, Edge View, Eyam, Derbyshire. *Pinnacles of Peak History*. 2nd ed., 1947.
Derbyshire Archaeological Society Journal. Annual, 1879-date. Contains many useful articles.
Derbyshire Miscellany: the bulletin of the local history section of the Derbyshire Archaeological Society. Quarterly, 1956-date.
EARWAKER, J. P. *East Cheshire*. 1877-80. The Author.
GUNSTONE, A. J. H. *An Archaeological gazetteer of Staffordshire*, Pt. 1 (1964). Part 2: The barrows (1965). Transactions of the North Staffordshire Field Club.

HEATHCOTE, J. P. *Birchover.* 1926. The Author.

HUNTER, J. *Hallamshire.* 1869. Virtue.

LYSONS, D., and S. Magna Britannia. Vol. 2, *Cheshire,* 1810; Vol. 5, *Derbyshire,* 1817.

Ministry of Public Building and Works. *Guide to Arbor Low,* by D. Thompson. 1963. H.M.S.O. (Includes notes on Hob Hurst's House, Eyam Moor circle and tumulus, and the Nine Ladies).

OZANNE, A. The Peak Dwellers (*Medieval Archaeology,* Vol. 6-7). 1962-3.

Victoria County Histories. *Derbyshire.* Vols. 1-2, 1905-07. O.U.P.; *Staffordshire.* Vols. 1 and 4, 1908, 1958. O.U.P.; *Yorkshire.* Vol. 2. O.U.P.

GEOLOGY

CHALLINOR, J. *North Staffordshire geology,* 3 parts. The Author, Broncastell, Capel Bangor, Aberystwyth, Dyfed.

COPE, F. W. *The Peak District, Derbyshire.* (*Geologists' Association Guides series*). New ed., 1965. Colchester, Benham.

DALE, E. *Scenery and geology of the Peak of Derbyshire.* 1900. Sampson Low.

DOWNIE, C., and NEVES, R., *eds. Geological Excursions in the Sheffield Region and the Peak District National Park.* 1967.

Geological Survey. *Geology of the Carboniferous Limestone, Yoredale Rocks and Millstone Grit of North Derbyshire,* by A. H. Green, etc. 1887; *Geology of the country around Holmfirth and Glossop,* by C. E. C. Bromehead, etc. 1933; *Geology of the country around Macclesfield, etc.,* by T. I. Pocock. 1906; *The Pennines and adjacent areas,* 3rd ed. by W. Edwards and F. M. Trotter. 1954.

JACKSON, J. W. The relation of the Edale Shales to the Carboniferous Limestone in North Derbyshire. (*Geological Magazine,* Vol. 62). 1925.

JACKSON, J. W. The succession below the Kinderscout Grit in North Derbyshire. (*Journal of the Manchester Geological Association,* Vol. 1). 1927.

MELLO, J. M. *Handbook of the geology of Derbyshire.* 2nd ed., 1891. Bemrose.

Quarterly Journal of the Geological Society of London. Parkinson, D. The stratigraphy of the Dovedale area. Vol. 105. Prentice, J. G. The Carboniferous limestone of the Manifold Valley region. Vol. 106.

NATURAL HISTORY

CLAPHAM, A. R., *ed. Flora of Derbyshire.* 1969. (Superseding Linton, 1903).

CONWAY, V. M. Ringinglow Bog, near Sheffield. (*Journal of Ecology,* Vol. 34). 1947.

GARNER, R. *Natural history of the county of Stafford, with supplement.* 1844.

MOSS, C. E. *Vegetation of the Peak District.* 1913. C.U.P.

North Staffordshire Field Club Transactions. Annual, 1866-1960. Central Reference Library, Hanley, Stoke-on-Trent.

PAINTER, W. H. Contribution to *Flora of Derbyshire,* 1889; supplement. 1902. Bell.

Peak Park Planning Board. Nature Trails series (Edale, Lathkill Dale, Padley Gorge).

PEARSALL, W. H. *Mountains and Moorlands.* 1950. Collins, London.

RIDGE, W. T. B. *Flora of North Staffordshire.* 1922-29. North Staffordshire Field Club.

SMITH, G. *Ferns of Derbyshire.* 1877. Bemrose.

SMITH, T. *Birds of Staffordshire.* 1930-38. North Staffordshire Field Club.

WHITLOCK, F. B. *Birds of Derbyshire.* 1893. Bemrose.

PLACE NAMES

CAMERON, K. *Place names of Derbyshire.* Vols. 1-3, 1959. C.U.P.

DUIGNAN, W. H. *Notes on Staffordshire place names.* 1902. O.U.P.

APPENDIX I

Scheduled Ancient Monuments in the Peak District National Park

1-in. O.S. Sheet
Grid Reference

CHESHIRE
(The parish name appears first)

BURIAL MOUNDS AND MEGALITHIC MONUMENTS

Lyme Handley, The Bow Stones	SJ 974814
Lyme Handley, two round barrows on Sponds Hill	SJ 970804
Macclesfield Forest, round barrow S.W. of earthwork on Toot Hill	SJ 971719
Rainow, round barrow W. of Blackrock Farm	SJ 958767
Rainow, round barrow S. of Blue Boar Farm	SJ 972764
Rainow, Yearn's Low, round barrow	SJ 964759

CROSSES

Lyme Handley, cross heads at Lyme Hall	SJ 966824
Wincle, Cleulow Cross	SJ 952674

MISCELLANEOUS

Macclesfield Forest, quadrilateral earthwork on Toot Hill	SJ 972721
Wincle, mound S.W. of Bartomley	SJ 965658

DERBYSHIRE
(The parish name appears first)

CAVES

Brassington, Harboro Cave	SK 243552

BURIAL MOUNDS AND MEGALITHIC MONUMENTS

Aldwark, Green Low, chambered round cairn	SK 232581
Bakewell, round barrow on Burton Moor	SK 201675
Ballidon, Minning Low, round barrow	SK 209573
Bamford, round barrows on Bamford Moor	SK 213850
Baslow and Bubnell, round barrow on Curbar Edge	SK 254756
Baslow and Bubnell, round barrows E. of Gardoms Edge	SK 278733
[1]Beeley, Hob Hurst's House, chambered barrow	SK 287693
Brampton, disc barrow in Rodknoll Plantation	SK 302698
Brushfield, Highfield round cairn	SK 169724
Chapel-en-le-Frith, Bull Ring and round barrow, Dove Holes	SK 079782
Chapel-en-le-Frith, Cow Low, round barrow	SK 066786
Chapel-en-le-Frith, Lady Low, round barrow	SK 066781
Chapel-en-le-Frith, Mag Low, round barrow	SK 079818
Chelmorton, Chelmorton Lows, round barrows	SK 115707
Chelmorton, Nether Low, round cairn	SK 109692
Derwent, Moscar Moor stone circle	SK 216869

[1]Monuments wholly or partly in the charge of the Secretary of State under the provisions of the Ancient Monuments Acts.

Eaton and Alsop, Cross Low, round barrow	SK 163555
Edale, Lord's Seat round barrow, Rushup Edge	SK 112835
Edensor, three round barrows on Calton Pastures	SK 234686
	SK 240683
	SK 241681
[1]Eyam, round barrow and stone circle on Eyam Moor	SK 226790
Froggatt, stone circle on Froggatt Edge	SK 250767
Gratton, Gratton Moor round cairn	SK 197608
Great Longstone, round barrow on Longstone Moor	SK 189732
Gt. Longstone, round cairn, 600 yards N.W. of Black Harry House	SK 198748
Great Longstone, Rolley Low, round barrow	SK 185736
Grindlow, Long Low, round barrow	SK 186773
Grindlow, Tup Low, round barrow	SK 187769
Harthill, Nine Stones, remains of stone circle	SK 227625
Hartington Middle Quarter, Benty Grange, round barrow	SK 146642
Hartington Middle Quarter, round barrows on Cronkston Low	SK 117663
Hartington Middle Quarter, round barrow S.W. of Parsley Hay Station	SK 146631
Hartington Middle Quarter, Pilsbury, round cairn	SK 121639
Hartington Middle Quarter, Vincent Knoll, round barrow (S.W. of Darley Farm)	SK 137635
Hartington Nether Quarter, Aleck Low round barrow	SK 175594
Hartington Nether Quarter, Liffs Low, round barrow	SK 153577
Hartington Town Quarter, End Low, round barrow	SK 156605
Hartington T.Q. (Town Quarter), Lean Low round cairn	SK 150622
Hartington Town Quarter, two round barrows at Moneystones	SK 150615
Hartington Town Quarter, Wolfscote Hill, round cairn	SK 137584
Hartington Upper Quarter, Great Low, round barrow	SK 107682
Hazlebadge, Cop Low, round barrow	SK 166792
Hazlebadge, round barrow 330 yds. N.E. of Hazlebadge Hall	SK 173802
Hayfield, Kinder Low, round barrow	SK 070867
Highlow, three round barrows on Highlow Bank	SK 212802
Holmesfield, stone circles and round barrows S. of Little Barbrook Reservoir	SK 278757
Hope Woodlands, long mound on Fair Banks, Ronksley Moor	SK 142974
[1]Middleton and Smerrill, Arbor Low earthen ring and stone circle, and Gib Hill, round barrow	SK 158633
	SK 160635
Middleton and Smerrill, Ringham Low, round barrow	SK 179619
Middleton & Smerrill, Smerrill Moor round cairn	SK 184608
Nether Haddon, round barrow ½ mile N.E. of Conksbury Bridge	SK 217662
Nether Haddon, round barrow ¼ mile S.E. of Conksbury Bridge	SK 215654
Newton Grange, Moat Low, round barrow	SK 155540
Offerton, round barrows and circular banks on Offerton Moor	SK 212805
Over Haddon, Grind Low, round barrow	SK 202670
Peak Forest, round barrow on Eldon Hill	SK 116811
Peak Forest, round barrow on Gautries Hill	SK 099810
Peak Forest, Sparrow Pit Barrow, round barrow 200 yds. N. of Harratt Grange	SK 099805
Sheldon, round barrow W. of Manor House	SK 169689
Stanton, Doll Tor stone circle	SK 238628
Stanton, group of chambered barrows, Stanton Moor	SK 248629
[1]Stanton, Nine Ladies stone circle, Stanton Moor	SK 248636
Taddington, Five Wells, chambered barrow	SK 124710
Tideswell, Tides Low, round barrow	SK 150780
Tissington, Rose Low, round barrow	SK 170527

[1]Monuments wholly or partly in the charge of the Secretary of State under the provisions of the Ancient Monuments Acts.

Wormhill, Wind Low, round barrow   SK 114751
Youlgreave, Bee Low, round cairn   SK 192647

CAMPS AND SETTLEMENTS

Ashford, Fin Cop earthwork   SK 175710
Bamford, earthwork on Bamford Moor   SK 213850
Baslow and Bubnell, village settlement E. of Gardoms Edge   SK 278433
Castleton, Mam Tor   SK 128837
Chapel-en-le-Frith, Combs Moss Camp   SK 055783
Charlesworth, Torside Castle   SK 077965
Edensor and Bakewell, Ballcross Camp   SK 227691
Great Hucklow, Burr Tor hill fort   SK 180783
Harthill, Castle Ring Camp   SK 221628

ROMAN REMAINS

Hope, Brough Roman fort   SK 181828
Outseats, Stanage Edge Roman road   SK 233849
Tideswell, Batham Gate Roman road   SK 133792

LINEAR EARTHWORKS

Bradwell, Grey Ditch   SK 173819
    SK 178816
    SK 182813

ECCLESIASTICAL BUILDINGS

Harthill, Cratcliffe Rocks, Hermitage and Crucifix   SK 227623

CROSSES

Bakewell, churchyard cross   SK 216685
Bakewell, cross shaft in churchyard from Two Dales, Darley   SK 284628
Baslow and Bubnell, Whibbersley Cross   SK 296728
Bradbourne, cross shaft near All Saints Church   SK 208527
[2]Chapel-en-le-Frith, market cross   SK 057807
Chapel-en-le-Frith, churchyard cross   SK 058808
Edale Cross   SK 078861
Eyam, churchyard cross   SK 219764
Foolow, village cross   SK 191767
Holmesfield, Lady's Cross, 460 yds. W. of Barbrook Bridge   SK 272728
Holmesfield, Fox Lane crosses, Ramsley Moor   SK 295749
Hope, two crosses in churchyard   SK 173834
Whaley Bridge, the Shall Cross   SK 017796
Wheston Cross   SK 132764

CASTLES

Bakewell, Castle Hill   SK 221688
[3]Castleton, Peveril Castle   SK 150826
Hartington, Pilsbury Castle Hills   SK 114638
Holmesfield, Castle Hill   SK 319776

OTHER SECULAR SITES AND BUILDINGS

Hathersage, Camp Green   SK 236819
Holmesfield, moated site N.N.E. of church   SK 322779
Nether Padley, cruck barn S. of Maynard Arms Hotel   SK 248783

BRIDGES

[2]Ashford Bridge   SK 199695

[2]Crown or Duchy property not in the charge of the Secretary of State.

[3]Crown or Duchy property wholly or partly in the charge of the Secretary of State.

Ashford, Sheepwash Bridge	SK 195695
Bakewell Bridge	SK 219686
Bakewell, Holm Bridge	SK 216689
Baslow Bridge	SK 296749
Beeley, One Arch Bridge	SK 261683
Hope Woodlands and Bradfield, reconstructed packhorse bridge from Derwent Hall	SK 180884
Rowsley, Rowsley Bridge	SK 257659

MISCELLANEOUS

Hathersage, enclosure in Lawrence Field	SK 254796
Hathersage, earthworks in Sheffield Plantation	SK 257783

STAFFORDSHIRE
(The parish name appears first)

CAVES

Wetton, Eldebush Cave	SK 099549

BURIAL MOUNDS AND MEGALITHIC MONUMENTS

Alstonfield, Pea Low, round barrow	SK 132565
Alstonfield, round barrow S. of Stanshope Pasture	SK 138537
Alstonfield, two round barrows E. of Stanshope	SK 132543
	SK 135542
Alstonfield, round barrow on Narrowdale Hill	SK 123572
Alstonfield, two round barrows on Gratton Hill	SK 131571
Blore with Swinscoe, Lady Low, round barrow	SK 139498
Blore with Swinscoe, Du Low, round barrow 600 feet W. of Waterings Farm	SK 121495
Blore with Swinscoe, round barrow 500 feet S. of Cliff Top, Swinscoe	SK 137482
Blore with Swinscoe, round barrow on Hazelton Hill	SK 126498
Blore with Swinscoe, round barrow S.W. of Blore	SK 133491
Blore with Swinscoe, Top Low, round barrow, Blore	SK 129491
Butterton, Town Low, round barrow E. of Lanehouse Farm	SK 084565
Fawfieldhead, two round barrows N. of The Low	SK 087631
	SK 089629
Grindon, round barrow ½ mile S.E. of village	SK 097539
	SK 082531
Grindon, two round barrows, Deepdale	SK 084530
Hollinsclough, round barrow N.E. of Coatestown	SK 063663
Ilam, Ilamtops Low, round barrow	SK 136526
Ilam, round barrow near Highfields Mine, S.W. of Stanshope	SK 120535
Ilam, round barrow W. of Damgate	SK 124532
Ilam, three round barrows N. of Castern Hall	SK 126528
	SK 129529
Ilam, three round barrows S. of Stanshope	SK 128536
	SK 128539
	SK 128538
Sheen, round barrow 700 yds. N. of Brund	SK 103619
Sheen, round cairn E. of Brund	SK 105612
Sheen, round cairn S. of Townend	SK 108605
Warslow and Elkstones, Blakelow round cairn	SK 087588
Warslow and Elkstones, Brownlow round cairn	SK 076581
Waterhouses, round cairn N. of Waterhouses	SK 084505
Waterhouses, round barrow ¼ mile N. of Latham Hall	SK 114495
Waterhouses, round barrow 500 ft. N. of Lower Green House	SK 108501
Waterhouses, four round barrows on Musden Low	SK 119500
Waterhouses, round barrow near Caltonmoor House	SK 113487

Wetton, two round barrows called Wetton Low	SK 110547
	SK 112547
Wetton, Top of Ecton, round barrow	SK 097573

CROSSES

Alstonfield, fragment of Saxon cross shaft in churchyard	SK 132533
Ilam, cross shaft in grounds of Ilam Hall	SK 129506
Ilam, two cross shafts in churchyard	SK 133507

OTHER SECULAR SITES AND BUILDINGS

Alstonfield, Charles Cotton Fishing House, Beresford Dale	SK 128593

BRIDGES

Alstonfield, Viator's Bridge	SK 140547
Ilam, St. Bertram's Bridge	SK 134506

YORKSHIRE
(The parish name appears first)

BURIAL MOUNDS AND MEGALITHIC MONUMENTS

Bradfield, Apronful of Stones, round barrow	SK 244946
Bradfield, group of round barrows near Ewden Beck	SK 237965
Bradfield, stone circle near Ewden Beck	SK 238966
Sheffield, group of round barrows N.W. of Burbage Bridge	SK 260809

CAMPS AND SETTLEMENTS

Sheffield, Carl Wark	SK 260815
Sheffield, Wincobank Camp	SK 377910

ROMAN REMAINS

Saddleworth, Castle Shaw, Roman forts	SE 999097

LINEAR EARTHWORKS

Bradfield, Bar Dike	SK 245945
	SK 247948
Bradfield, earthwork on Moor Side near Ewden Beck	SK 230962
	SK 238964
Roman Ridge, Sheffield: section 600 yds. long between Jenkin Lane and Tyler Street	SK 385914
Roman Ridge, Sheffield: section 180 yds. long on S.E. slopes of Wincobank Hill	SK 381910

CASTLES

Bradfield, Bailey Hill	SK 266927
Bradfield, Castle Hill	SK 272924

OTHER SECULAR SITES AND BUILDINGS

Sheffield, Manor Lodge	SK 376865

ECCLESIASTICAL BUILDINGS

Sheffield, Beauchief Abbey	SK 335819

APPENDIX II

Some Useful Addresses

ANGLING

Trent District Anglers' Consultative Association, 56 Ward Street, Derby.

See also the chapter on Sport in the Peak. In addition a duplicated leaflet on Fishing is available from the Peak Park Joint Planning Board on receipt of a large stamped addressed envelope.

ARCHAEOLOGICAL, HISTORICAL AND NATURAL HISTORY SOCIETIES

Bakewell Historical Society
Hon. Sec.: Mrs. D. L. Rylands, Parsonage Croft, Bakewell
Buxton Archaeological and Natural History Society
Hon. Secs.: I. H. Morten, O.B.E., and E. Bradbury, The Plex Farm, Burbage, Buxton, Derbyshire
Buxton Field Club
Hon. Sec.: D. T. Wilks, 7 Trenchard Drive, Harpur Hill, Buxton
Council for Nature
Zoological Gardens, Regent's Park, London NW1
Derbyshire Archaeological Society
Hon. Sec.: M. A. B. Mallender, 35 St. Mary's Gate, Derby DE3 2BB
Derbyshire Ornithological Society
Hon. Sec.: R. H. Appleby, 25 Rykneld Way, Littleover, Derby
Hunter Archaeological Society
Hon. Sec.: F. L. Preston, Grove Cottage, Margate Grove, Rotherham
Leek and District Field Club
Hon. Sec.: Miss D. Hill, 6 Newcastle Road, Leek, Staffs
Macclesfield and District Field Club
Hon. Sec.: Miss F. M. Chapman, 68 Chestergate, Macclesfield
North Staffordshire Field Club
Hon. Sec.: R. A. Tribbeck, Department of Chemistry, North Staffordshire Polytechnic, College Road, Stoke-on-Trent
Peak District Mines Historical Society
Hon. Sec.: P. Naylor, 12 Rowley Gardens, Littleover, Derby
Sorby Natural History Society
Hon. Sec.: Miss June Robinson, 17 Winchester Avenue, Sheffield S10 4EA.

AUTOMOBILE ASSOCIATION
Headquarters: Basing View, Basingstoke, Hants RG21 2EA
Manchester Area: Fanum House, York Street, Manchester 2
Sheffield Area: 18 Paradise Square, Sheffield 1
Stoke-on-Trent: Normeir Buildings, St. Andrew's Square, Stoke-on-Trent

BRITISH CANOE UNION
General Secretary, 70 Brompton Road, London SW3 1HE

BRITISH TOURIST AUTHORITY
64/65 St. James's Street, Piccadilly, London SW1A 1NF

CAMPING CLUB OF GREAT BRITAIN AND IRELAND
Headquarters: 11 Lower Grosvenor Place, London SW1

CARAVAN CLUB OF GREAT BRITAIN AND IRELAND
Headquarters: 65 South Molton Street, London W1Y 2AB

COUNCIL FOR NATURE
Headquarters: Zoological Gardens, Regent's Park, London NW1 4RY

COUNCIL FOR THE PROTECTION OF RURAL ENGLAND
Headquarters: 4 Hobart Place, London SW1 0HY
Sheffield and Peak District Branch
Hon. Sec.: Mrs. G. G. Haythornthwaite, 22 Endcliffe Crescent, Sheffield S10 3EF
Cheshire Branch
Hon. Sec.: R. H. C. Black, Bridgegate House, Lower Bridge Street, Chester
Staffordshire Branch
Hon. Sec.: D. W. Riley, over Mottram's shop, Martin Street, Stafford

COUNTRY-WIDE HOLIDAYS ASSOCIATION
Headquarters: Birch Heys, Cromwell Range, Manchester 14
Centre: Moor Gate, Hope, via Sheffield

CYCLISTS' TOURING CLUB
Cotterell House, 69 Meadrow, Godalming, Surrey

GLIDING
British Gliding Association, Artillery Mansions, 75 Victoria Street, London SW1
Derbyshire and Lancashire Gliding Club, Camphill, Great Hucklow, Tideswell, Buxton

MOUNTAIN RESCUE POSTS

These are listed in the annual booklet of the Mountain Rescue Committee.
Hon. Sec.: H. K. Hartley, 9 Milldale Avenue, Temple Meads, Buxton.
Booklet on sale from the Peak Park Joint Planning Board

MOUNTAINEERING

The British Mountaineering Council, 70 Brompton Road, London SW3 1HE
B.M.C. Peak District Committee
Hon. Sec.: R. H. Jeal, 7 Stanton Avenue, Belper, Derbyshire DE5 1EE

NATIONAL EQUESTRIAN CENTRE

Stoneleigh, Kenilworth, Warwickshire

THE NATIONAL TRUST

Headquarters: 42 Queen Anne's Gate, London SW1H 9AS

NATURALISTS' TRUSTS

Cheshire Conservation Trust
Administrative Officer: Wing Commander E. W. D. Roy, O.B.E., D.F.C., 2 Pear Tree Lane, Acton Bridge, Northwich, Cheshire CW8 3QR
Derbyshire Naturalists' Trust
Hon. Sec.: R. H. Appleby, 25 Rykneld Way, Littleover, Derby DE3 7AT
Staffordshire Nature Conservation Trust
Hon. Sec.: J. Taylor, 5 Harrowby Drive, Newcastle, Stoke-on-Trent
Yorkshire Naturalists' Trust
20 Castlegate, York YO1 1RP

NATURE CONSERVANCY COUNCIL

Headquarters: 19 Belgrave Square, London SW1X 8PY
Midland Regional Office: Attingham Park, Shrewsbury, Salop SY4 4TW

OUTWARD BOUND TRUST

Iddesleigh House, Caxton Street, London SW1

PEAK AND NORTHERN FOOTPATHS SOCIETY

General Secretary: E. A. W. Newton, 79 Taunton Road, Ashton-under-Lyne, Lancs

PEAK PARK JOINT PLANNING BOARD

National Park Office, Baslow Road, Bakewell, Derbyshire DE4 1AE. Tel. Bakewell 2881
National Park Information Centres:
Market Hall, Bridge Street, Bakewell (Tel. 3227)
St. Ann's Well, The Crescent, Buxton (Tel. 5106)
Castle Street, Castleton (Tel. Hope Valley 20679)
Field Head, Edale (Tel. 207)

POTHOLING

British Association of Caving Instructors
Hon. Sec., 5 St. Paul's Street, Leeds LS1 2NQ
British Cave Research Association
Hon. Sec.: D. Judson, Bethel Green, Calderbrook Road, Little-
borough, Lancashire OL15 9ND
National Caving Association
Hon. Sec.: c/o Department of Geography, The University, P.O. Box
363, Birmingham B15 3TT
Derbyshire Caving Association
Hon. Sec.: Mrs. J. E. Potts, 3 Greenway, Hulland Ward, Derby
DE6 3FE

RAMBLERS' ASSOCIATION

Headquarters: 1/4 Crawford Mews, London W1H 1PT
Derbyshire Area
Hon. Sec.: Mrs. D. West, 17 Moncrieff Crescent, Chaddesden, Derby
DE2 4NR
Matlock and Bakewell Group
Hon. Sec.: Mrs. M. R. Treece, Dene Cottage, Alport, near Bakewell,
Derbyshire
Manchester Area
Hon. Sec.: Miss R. Irlam, 4 Sunningdale Road, Urmston, Manchester
M31 1DG
North Staffordshire Area
Hon. Sec.: W. G. Oakden, 79 Trent Valley Road, Penkhull, Stoke-on-
Trent
Sheffield District
Hon. Sec.: W. N. Norton, 53 Dalewood Avenue, Sheffield 8

ROYAL AUTOMOBILE CLUB

Headquarters: 85 Pall Mall, London SW1
Manchester Area: 135 Dickinson Road, Manchester 14

SKI-ING

National Ski Federation of Great Britain, 118 Eaton Square, London
SW1
East Midland Ski Association, 25 St. Ann's Well Road, Nottingham
NG3 1ER

SPORTS COUNCIL

70 Brompton Road, London SW3 1EX

YOUTH HOSTELS ASSOCIATION

Headquarters: Trevelyan House, 8 St. Stephens Hill, St. Albans, Herts
Peak Regional Office
Secretary: D. R. Allison, Crompton Chambers, Dale Road, Matlock, Derbyshire

HOSTELS

Bakewell: The Warden, Fly Hill, Bakewell, Derbyshire (G.R. SK 215685)

Bretton: (Open Sat. and Bank Holidays only) Bookings, stating name of hostel, to Mrs. Stones, 4 Roach Road, Sheffield. Tel. Sheffield 66677. (G.R. SK 200780)

Buxton: The Warden, Sherbrook Lodge, Harpur Hill Road, Buxton, Derbyshire (G.R. SK 063722)

Castleton: The Warden, Castleton Hall, Castleton, via Sheffield (G.R. SK 150828)

Crowden-in-Longdendale: (Closed October to mid-March). A Peak National Park Hostel open to members of the public, with accommodation available to Y.H.A. members at Y.H.A. charges. The Warden, Peak National Park Hostel, Crowden, Hadfield, Hyde, Cheshire. Tel. Glossop 2135 (G.R. SK 073993)

Edale: The Warden, Rowland Cote, Nether Booth, Edale, via Sheffield (G.R. SK 140866)

Elton: The Warden, Elton Old Hall, Main Street, Elton, nr. Matlock, Derbyshire (G.R. SK 224608)

Eyam: The Warden, Edge Road, Eyam, Derbyshire (G.R. SK 221767)

Hagg Farm, Ashopton, near Bamford: A Peak National Park Mountain Hostel and Camp Site open to all members of the public. The Warden, Hagg Farm, Ashopton, Bamford, Sheffield S30 2BJ (Tel. Bamford 594)

Hartington: The Warden, Hartington Hall, Hartington, nr. Buxton, Derbyshire (G.R. SK 132603)

Hathersage: The Warden, Castleton Road, Hathersage, Sheffield (G.R. SK 229816)

Ilam Hall: The Warden, Ilam Hall, Ashbourne, Derbyshire (G.R. SK 131506)

Langsett: The Warden, Langsett, Stocksbridge, Sheffield (G.R. SE 211005)

Matlock Bath: The Warden, Youth Hostel, Brunswood Road, Matlock Bath, Derbyshire (G.R. SK 296585)

Ravenstor: The Warden, Ravenstor, Miller's Dale, Buxton, Derbyshire (G.R. SK 152732)

Shining Cliff: (Open Sat. and Bank Holidays only) Shining Cliff Woods, near Ambergate, Derbyshire. Bookings to Y.H.A., 3 Leopold Street, Derbyshire (G.R. SK 334522)

Windgather Cottage: The Warden, Windgather Cottage, Kettleshulme, Whaley Bridge, Stockport, Cheshire (G.R. SJ 993758)

INDEX

Index

OTHER GUIDES
IN THE NATIONAL PARK SERIES

Obtainable from
HER MAJESTY'S STATIONERY OFFICE
at the addresses on cover page iv
or through booksellers

The Country Code

GUARD AGAINST FIRE RISKS

Plantations, woodlands and heaths are highly inflammable: every year acres burn because of casually dropped matches, cigarette ends or pipe ash.

FASTEN ALL GATES

Even if you found them open. Animals can't be told to stay where they're put. A gate left open invites them to wander, a danger to themselves, to crops and to traffic.

KEEP DOGS UNDER PROPER CONTROL

Farmers have good reason to regard visiting dogs as pests; in the country a civilised town dog can become a savage. Keep your dog on a lead where-ever there is livestock about, also on country roads.

KEEP TO PATHS ACROSS FARM LAND

Crops can be ruined by people's feet. Remember that grass is a valuable crop too, in some cases the only one on the farm. Flattened corn or hay is very difficult to harvest.

AVOID DAMAGING FENCES, HEDGES AND WALLS

They are expensive items in the farmer's economy; repairs are costly and use scarce labour. Keep to recognised routes, using gates and stiles.

LEAVE NO LITTER

All litter is unsightly, and some is dangerous as well. Take litter home for disposal; in the country it costs a lot to collect it.

SAFEGUARD WATER SUPPLIES

Your chosen walk may well cross a catchment area for the water supply of millions. Avoid polluting it in any way. Never interfere with cattle troughs.

The Country Code

PROTECT WILD LIFE, WILD PLANTS AND TREES

Wild life is best observed, not collected. To pick or uproot flowers, carve trees and rocks, or disturb wild animals and birds, destroys other people's pleasure as well.

GO CAREFULLY ON COUNTRY ROADS

Country roads have special dangers: blind corners, high banks and hedges, slow-moving tractors and farm machinery or animals. Motorists should reduce their speed and take extra care, walkers should keep to the right, facing oncoming traffic.

RESPECT THE LIFE OF THE COUNTRYSIDE

Set a good example and try to fit in with the life and work of the countryside. This way good relations are preserved, and those who follow are not regarded as enemies.

Printed in England for Her Majesty's Stationery Office by
McCorquodale & Co. Ltd., Printers, London
HM 6712   Dd. 504270   K80   5/75   McC.   3305

HER MAJESTY'S STATIONERY OFFICE

Government Bookshops

49 High Holborn, London WC1 6HB
13a Castle Street, Edinburgh EH2 3AR
41 The Hayes, Cardiff CF1 1JW
Brazennose Street, Manchester M60 8AS
Southey House, Wine Street, Bristol BS1 2BQ
258 Broad Street, Birmingham B1 2HE
80 Chichester Street, Belfast BT1 4JY

*Government Publications are also available
through booksellers*

ISBN 0 11 700497 9